Environmental Problem Solving

Theory, Practice and Possibilities in Environmental Education

Editors:

Lisa V. Bardwell
Martha C. Monroe
Margaret T. Tudor

NAAEE

NORTH AMERICAN
ASSOCIATION FOR
ENVIRONMENTAL
EDUCATION

CURR
GE
70
E38
1994

Environmental Problem Solving: Theory, Practice, and Possibilities in Environmental Education

ISBN 1-884-008-13-5

 Printed on recycled paper.

ACKNOWLEDGEMENTS

We want to express our sincere thanks to the many members of the North American Association for Environmental Education who contributed to this monograph, and to the National Consortium for Environmental Education and Training for supplementary funding.

Judy Braus, as chair of the Publications Committee, facilitated the molding of an idea into a monograph. The careful review of the draft manuscript by Cliff Knapp, Lori Mann, and Linda Manning resulted in a number of substantive changes and greatly improved its readability.

The following members responded to an invitation to describe their involvement in teaching problem solving skills. By March, 1992, 12 people submitted descriptions of their programs, and 13 members had completed a short survey looking at teaching environmental problem solving. Their insights were used to frame Chapter 3 and can be found in the Appendix.

Janet Carrier Ady	Janis Albright-Burton
Ivan Baugh	Anne Camozzi
Michael J. Cohen	Peter Blaze Corcoran and Eric Sievers
Carol Fialkowski	Susan Jacobson and Rafael Robles
Ruth Jacquot	Dan Kowal
Martin Ogle	Melva Okun
Zyg Plater	Lucie Sauvé and Armel Boutard
Robert Steelquist	Alice Steinbach

We have gained from the wisdom of our mentors and colleagues along the way, and wish to give them credit for helping to shape our ideas, questions, and curiosities about problem solving:

    Stephen and Rachel Kaplan
    William B. Stapp
    Raymond DeYoung

The authors of the various approaches warrant our deepest thanks, not only for their cooperation and ultimate patience with the development of this monograph, but most of all, for their ongoing contributions to the EE field.

William F. Hammond	Harold R. Hungerford
Ian Robottom	William B. Stapp
Trudi L. Volk	Arjen E.J. Wals
Austin A. Winther	

Finally, the efforts of Annabelle McInlay, Kira Wilkins James, and Peggy Re greatly improved the quality and appearance of this manuscript.

Lisa V. Bardwell   *Martha C. Monroe*   *Margaret T. Tudor*

Environmental Problem Solving:
Theory, Practice, and Possibilities in Environmental Education

TABLE OF CONTENTS

APPENDIX
FULL TEXT OF PRACTITIONER DESCRIPTIONS

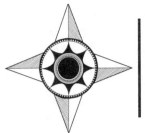

INTRODUCTION

E ach year, I look for a local environmental issue to use as a model for environmental problem solving. I want students to become aware of the issue, gain information, and participate in simulations that deal with possible solutions before selecting their actions. Students become involved as environmental political activists, community educators, or agents for changing behaviors.

In the spring of 1989, we focused on the community landfill. For several months, classes followed media coverage of the Michigan Department of Natural Resources'(DNR) concern that the local sanitary landfill was unsafe and should possibly be shut down. There were many heated meetings between the Chelsea Village Council and DNR officials. We read and posted newspaper articles and letters to the editor in the classroom.

I invited an environmental health specialist from the county Department of Health to speak. He told the class that the department had received reports of leaks of toxic substances appearing in wells adjacent to the landfill. We arranged field trips to the landfill. Both the local landfill manager and DNR officials were present and helped us understand how landfills operate and what the concerns were at the site. Students also saw how the site related to adjacent private property and state owned wetlands.

Next, each student, individually or in a group, worked on an independent project. Each project was chosen with consideration for the interests, talents, and abilities of the individual student. They included letters to government officials and editors of local newspapers; posters urging the community to recycle and eliminate unnecessary solid and toxic wastes, children's stories about toxic and solid-waste concerns, political cartoons, involvement in recycling, and using alternative non-toxic substances in school and at home.

We used aerial photographs of the landfill site and surrounding area for an in-class simulation. Groups of students developed land use plans for the sanitary landfill site if and when it closed. The plans chosen as "best" by student "village council" members were presented at a Village Council meeting. Members of the Village Council listened to the proposals with interest and asked the students to leave their plans for consideration. The community has since implemented recycling programs for solid and toxic waste.

Today, many former students have environmentally related jobs and professions. Former students contact me for environmental information or to discuss what has happened to "their" issue. Many of my current students, their offspring, refer to environmental activities in which their parents participated as students. These parents have been supportive of environmental problem solving activities in classes and frequently become involved themselves.

Alice Steinbach has taught at Beach Middle School in Chelsea, Michigan, for 30 years. The exercises that she designed for her class, while not unique, are a wonderful example of how environmental problem solving can occur in the classroom. Her efforts represent one way of helping learners work through the basic phases of environmental problem solving:

1. Exploring and defining the problem

2. Searching for and identifying solutions

3. Implementing and evaluating actions

One aspect of addressing any environmental problem is *figuring out what is going on*. One explores the issue from several perspectives, perhaps collecting information and reactions firsthand or researching existing records. Alice focused on a real concern, a community issue, and had her students build an understanding of the problem by gathering information from a range of sources, listening to guest speakers, and taking a field trip.

A second phase involves *figuring out what to do*. Rather than opting for the first solution that comes to mind, one tries to understand the problem well enough to imagine the outcome of several alternate solutions. In her classroom, Alice did not have students come up with solutions, but instead gave them a range of projects that helped them use their emerging understanding and skills to try out different alternatives.

The third phase of environmental problem solving involves *actually doing something* that will lead toward a solution. Many of the projects of Alice's students focused on action. Furthermore, the land use plans they developed actually helped contribute to their community's efforts.

Engaging classrooms in a problem solving process is not commonplace. Nor is doing it well easy. Students need to understand and explore the issues. They need experience in the areas of analyzing and collecting information, working with people, predicting outcomes, and planning actions. What a teacher does and how much effort is placed on each of these components will vary based on the issue, the community, and the skills and needs of the students.

While there is no set procedure for teaching environmental problem solving skills, there are guidelines, examples, and models that can help teachers improve opportunities for building these skills among their students. This monograph is one such resource for educators who wish to explore this critically important field. The path is not thoroughly mapped and predictable, but neither is it a complete unknown. There is room for new ideas and experiments, more examples and models, and more practice.

The monograph consists of five parts:

1. Chapter 1 presents a psychological perspective on problem solving and its implications for teaching problem solving skills in an interdisciplinary arena.

2. Chapter 2 presents four approaches to developing environmental problem solving abilities developed by several environmental education practitioners and researchers in North America and Australia. The editors' commentary ties these models to the themes raised in Chapter 1.

3. Chapter 3 is a discussion of some of the common strands in the experiences of environmental education practitioners. Members of the North American Association for Environmental Education contributed to this analysis, which also parallels the themes raised in the first chapter.

4. Chapter 4 provides classroom activities that teachers could use to supplement their exploration of local environmental issues.

5. The Appendix includes descriptions of the programs used to compile Chapter 3.

The monograph is the result of collaboration between the editors—Lisa Bardwell, Martha Monroe and Margaret Tudor—and contributors. It is in no way definitive; it is another contribution to the ongoing dialogue about how we can better promote environmental understanding and problem solving skills in our citizenry.

PROBLEM SOLVING THROUGH A COGNITIVE LENS

Lisa V. Bardwell
Margaret T. Tudor

Any environmental educator knows teaching about environmental problems and their solutions is an incredibly challenging endeavor. It entails both teaching the science of an issue and helping learners bring to that understanding a recognition of social, political, and cultural factors. Since environmental problems are rarely solved by individuals working alone, learners need to be able to communicate and work with others. They must learn to identify their own values and priorities, and to respect those of others. Furthermore, because doing something about the problem is part of environmental education's mission, they need skills, confidence, and motivation to take effective action.

This chapter sets the stage for looking at four perspectives on teaching environmental problem solving and descriptions of educators' successes in teaching these skills. You may find it useful to read this chapter first, focusing on its major points, then to revisit it after reading the others. This chapter looks at the following:

1. **The challenging, often frustrating nature of environmental problems.**
   Environmental problems are complex. They rarely have one right answer. Any effort to solve them must incorporate scientific, political, economic, cultural, and technological considerations.

2. **The realities and limitations of how people use information and solve problems.**
   Cognitive maps and people's need to make sense of and be able to act on their understanding play an important role in how we define and solve problems.

3. **The traditional problem solving literature for clues about environmental problem solving.**
   Research on the different problem-solving processes of experts and novices suggests some strategies and skills environmental educators may be able to encourage.

4. **How to use this information to improve teaching environmental problem solving.**
   We focus on three aspects: familiarity, structure, and flexibility. Students need familiarity with content; they need to be able to structure and organize their understanding so they can be flexible in how they manipulate and "play" with different perspectives and options.

The Nature of Environmental Problems

For several decades, environmental education has been dedicated to developing a "world population aware of, and concerned about the total environment and its associated problems, one which has the knowledge, attitudes, motivations, commitments, and skills to work individually and collectively toward solutions of current problems and the prevention of new ones" (UNESCO, 1978). While the field has made a number of inroads, environmental education and environmental problem solving are only beginning to attract far-reaching public attention.

One reason this effort has proven so challenging relates to the very nature of environmental problems. Many of the problems we teach students to solve in school (or use to measure their problem solving abilities on the Standard Achievement Tests) are simple, "tame" problems. In eighth grade mathematics, for example, a word problem often has a single, correct answer. One is either right or wrong.

Environmental problems are not so simple. Computing the temperature change in the event of global warming is not a simple math problem. Nor is figuring out what the implications of any such calculation might mean! Students rarely wrestle with these kinds of "wicked" problems in the classroom. There are many dimensions of the complexity that make an environmental problem difficult to solve:

First, these issues are multidisciplinary. They require that we integrate the science, social science, technological, and personal domains. Each of these areas has a different perspective and a different way of thinking about problems. How we share our understanding of these perspectives is another challenge presented by complex problems.

Second, we must consider a number of ways to look at these problems. For example, while we can establish and agree on the fecal coliform count in a local watershed and, perhaps, even find its source, what we decide to *do* with this information presents a number of possibilities. Is the concern one of monitoring the condition of the river; ensuring public health? Depending on our problem definition, we may decide to restrict access to the river, write letters to city officials, initiate a watershed clean-up effort, or build a new water treatment plant. Each solution presents an array of options, and each option precipitates its own problems or, more optimistically, challenges.

Third, environmental issues are plagued with uncertainty. The information needed to evaluate some options may not exist. Or, if available, the facts may be contradictory. Furthermore, we often cannot predict how our decisions will play out in the future. In the 1950's, the invention of CFCs addressed a number of problems. They were inert gases and therefore long lasting. They were extremely versatile and effective as coolants, cleaning agents, and aerosols. Who would have guessed that these very characteristics could have had such a dramatic impact on the atmosphere?

Fourth, environmental decisions require group interaction; it is unlikely that only one person will make any decision. With that interaction comes the increased need for effective communication, leadership, and a process for working through conflicts and value differences.

Finally, the solutions themselves are often controversial and value laden. Embedded in every solution are assumptions and expectations that may not be shared by everyone. Successful implementation will hinge as much on public response and commitment as it will on careful planning and scientific realities.

On one hand, it is a wonder we think we can tackle environmental problems. On the other, it is imperative that we try. Educators can play a tremendously important role in preparing learners to participate in solving these particularly "wicked" problems. Critical to that effort is an understanding about how humans manage information and solve problems.

Humans As Problem Solvers

In many respects, environmental problems are people problems. At their most basic, they result from impacts of human behavior. Both problem prevention and viable solutions hinge on the effective use of human ingenuity and capabilities, and on a realistic understanding of our cognitive limitations.

From a cognitive perspective, humans have two basic information needs—to make sense of what is happening around them and to be able to explore and be involved in that world (Kaplan & Kaplan, 1982). Problem solving represents a crossroads of these two concerns; it involves building an understanding so that we can make predictions and decide what to do.

Making Sense and Understanding
Students, like all of us, do not absorb everything presented to them. Furthermore, they seem to have a marvelous propensity for selecting, interpreting, and organizing information in the most unexpected ways! In reality, this process is not as haphazard as it may seem.

Humans are mentally incapable of taking in all the information presented to them. They can hold between three and seven working concepts in their heads at once (Mandler, 1975). So, rather than retaining everything, we tend to chunk some information and selectively ignore the rest. These chunks of information, or cognitive maps, are based on our experiences. We more easily take in information that fits with or augments these maps.

Cognitive maps, then, provide an efficient organization that accommodates our limited information-processing capabilities. We use them to access very rapidly, often almost automatically, a reservoir of organized information to interpret and respond to what is happening. These mental maps *are* our understanding of the world.

Learning is about building on and expanding these maps. As we experience how different ideas, facts, and events connect, we build hierarchies, maps at different levels of abstraction. At the most basic levels, for example, we learn to recognize categories of things. Children recognize "bird" as a concept that describes creatures that may vary tremendously in coloration, behavior, and size. Over time, their associations can become increasingly abstract—birds are alive and therefore share similar processes with us (e.g., eating and sleeping); airplanes are sort of like birds because they fly. Our ability to equate birds and their ability to fly away with the concept of freedom is very abstract indeed.

Another example: we might have a thorough knowledge of a local natural history museum—where to find the dinosaurs, the butterfly exhibit, and the dioramas. With experience, we also develop a higher level map of *how* to find dinosaurs and butterflies in another natural history museum, and more generally, *how to behave and what to look* for in any kind of museum. Having these different levels of maps, we can generalize and see patterns. Thus, our understanding goes beyond the here and now. We can strategize, compare, and predict.

Exploration and Involvement

These cognitive maps are extremely important to us; they shape how we see our world and they guide our actions. We have only to think of how stubbornly people stick to what they believe to recognize that humans are very invested in their mental maps. Our existing maps give us someplace to start. Rather than build a new map every time we encounter a novel situation, we first try to use the maps we already have. A novice computer user, for example, may treat the computer like a typewriter and hit "return" at the end of every line. That recognition is part of what has made Macintosh computers so popular. The design is user-friendly because it converts arcane computer commands into words and functions we do every day. With a Macintosh, for example, users discard a file by putting it in the "trash."

One of the advantages of having mental maps is that they facilitate action. With a preexisting conception of a situation, we can look ahead, predict some possible outcomes, and anticipate appropriate behavior. When the maps we have do not fit or if they conflict with something new, we enter the realm of problem solving. Because it is uncomfortable to remain in a state of indecision, we opt for some kind of action. If we feel confident, the incongruity may spark a curious exploration and intense learning. If that discomfort leads to confusion or embarrassment, it may elicit very different, less helpful reactions such as anger, frustration, denial, and helplessness.

This discomfort with indecision and the inclination toward action in the real world become problematic when the definition process happens too quickly. In our haste to get to a solution, we define the problem inadequately or inaccurately. In short, we do a poor job of problem solving. We overlook possibilities because we miscast a new situation into the mold of a familiar one. It is difficult for us to see things through completely new eyes.

These informational needs have important implications given the multidisciplinary nature of environmental problems. As most educators know, unless explicitly prompted to use different domains of knowledge, students tend to rely on the familiar (Solomon, 1984). In most cases, this means students work from their personal perspective rather than approaching the problem from a scientific, social science, or political vantage (Fleming, 1986). The educational challenge, then, is to provide learners with the exposure and experience they need to be familiar enough with other domains to actually call on them. They need to have strategies for gaining and managing useful information, and for fitting that new knowledge into what they already know.

Problem Solving From a Psychological Perspective

What happens when these humans face a problem? Our definition of problem solving is very broad; it is what we do to figure out what to do next. Solving a math problem, deciding what movie to see, strategizing one's next chess move, organizing a class, and dealing with hazardous wastes all require problem solving skills. However, they differ along a number of dimensions—how simple or complex they are, how many people are involved, and the real-world implications of their solutions.

Most of the theoretical work in problem solving has focused on the simple, "tame," or well-structured problems typically encountered in schools (e.g., logic, physics, chemistry, and math). For these, the problem is usually well defined and it is obvious when one has reached a solution. While the process may be the same, solving complex, "wicked," or ill-structured problems emphasizes different parts of that process. Much of our understanding about these problems has come from comparisons of how experts and novices approach them.

A Characterization of Problem Solving

In its most simple form, problem solving is a multistaged process that entails

1. **Exploring and defining the problem:** building a representation or understanding of the problem and establishing some initial criteria to define the goal.

2. **Searching for and identifying solutions:** accessing and gathering information, doing experiments, or proceeding by trial and error to establish possible paths that lead from start to goal.

3. **Implementing an action and evaluating progress:** comparing initial goals to the chosen solution and monitoring that solution.

The typical characterization of problem solving is as a linear process. The start signifies the present situation, the goal is where one hopes to end. Problem solving is the search for a connecting path, i.e., the steps necessary to get from start to goal (Posner, 1973, Figure 1:1).

FIGURE 1:1
Linear Depiction
(Posner, 1973)

Start ——— P – A – T – H ⟶ Goal

Such a simple characterization belies the complexity of most problems, even ones that are not the obviously complex environmental problems. Real-world problems aren't quite so straightforward. There may be a number of starts that define the problem in different ways, several paths to test out, and sometimes more than one adequate solution.

A more useful conceptualization would view the path as the route between the problem and solution spaces (Figure 1:2). Slightly different starts (or problem definitions) will lead in different directions. Rather than having a direct sequence of steps to the goal, there may be subgoals, which break the problem into small parts. After getting stuck at a point that does not lead to the ultimate goal, one may return to the problem space (now understanding the problem a little differently) and begin again.

FIGURE 1:2
Spatial Depiction
(based on Kaplan
& Kaplan, 1982)

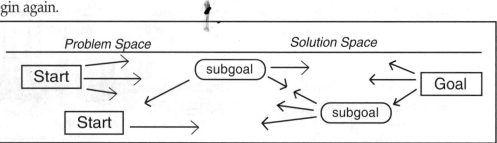

For example (Figure 1:3), if a local landfill is reaching capacity, one start might define the problem as "we have too much trash"; another might work from the assessment that "we don't have enough space to put our waste." While the goal for both is related to managing waste, the solutions and approaches could be very different.[1] For the first start, a possible solution might focus on reducing the amount of trash produced and slowing inputs into the facility, with subgoals of instituting a composting program or encouraging source reduction. The other start would mean locating and financing the purchase of a new site (see Futures Wheel activity in Chapter 4).

Effective problem solving is iterative. We play with several problem definitions and crisscross the boundary between the problem and solution spaces to see where various paths lead. Suppose, for example, someone suggests an incinerator, and another, the option of imposing a bag fee. A foray into the solution space to look at the implications and costs of these options can facilitate overall deliberation on the issue. This depth of understanding, however, is possible only when the problem space provides several representations.

---

[1] The National Issues Forum and the Environmental Issues Forum materials provide an excellent introductory context for looking at different problem perceptions related to air pollution, energy, solid waste, and wetlands protection. Other topic books should be forthcoming from NAAEE.

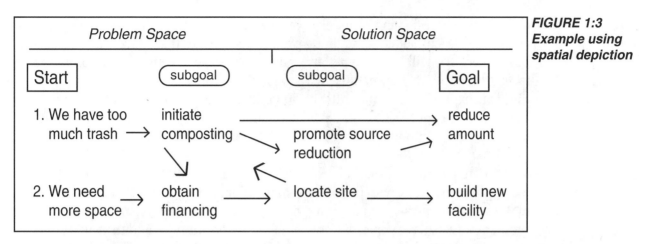

Much of the problem solving literature examines the solution and evaluation phases of problem solving. However, it is the start, the problem definition, which most profoundly affects where we end up (Sanford, 1985).

> The initial representation of a problem may be the most crucial single factor governing the likelihood of problem solution.... Whether a problem is solved or not, and how long the solution will take depend a great deal upon the initial representation (Posner, 1973, p. 149).

What may seem to be an insurmountable problem in one representation, may have an implicit solution when viewed from another vantage. For example, graffiti is considered a fairly undesirable urban problem. A typical problem definition might be "how can we get people to stop writing on walls"? From this view of the problem, laws are enacted against it, city crews spend large amounts of money and time cleaning it up, and engineers create more difficult surfaces on which to write. The solutions look considerably different if we view graffiti as a form of expression or even misplaced art. In this case we might provide surfaces for people to speak their minds legitimately.

This perspective speaks to the great importance of exploring the problem space and understanding the problem from various viewpoints (Step 1). The process of arriving at a solution (Step 2) is achieved after conceptualizing several potential paths to the goal, and perhaps by modeling or imagining the solution. The third step of environmental problem solving involves implementing the solution and practicing the skills of communicating, persuading, and strategizing for political or personal change. This step could result in difficulties or failure and contribute to a more realistic understanding of the problem and solution spaces. Learners may have to rework the solution or even revisit their definition of the problem. Problem solving is a process which continues even with one's new solution, for with wicked problems, every solution brings with it a new set of problems.

Elements of Effective Problem Solving

Clearly, a mandate for good problem solving is being able to come up with an adequate problem definition. To do that, one has to have enough familiarity with the problem to be able to stay in the problem space. In terms of the discussion above, this means having a model or cognitive map to shape that space. The more adequate one's understanding of the problem, the richer that space will be and the more likely one will be to see patterns and possible paths instead of disjointed facts. In common parlance, those with the more adequate understanding of something are experts[2]; those with little or no familiarity are novices. Not surprisingly, a comparison of approaches used by experts and novice problem solvers provides important clues into ways we might help learners become better problem solvers.

Experts are people with enough experience and familiarity with a certain field to more efficiently work with the subject matter. For example, novice/expert research in the sciences (physics, engineering, math, genetics) has demonstrated that skilled problem solvers have superior knowledge of important rules and principles that they appropriately apply to a problem (Gagne, 1985). They also represent the problems in ways which enable them to more effectively explore the problem space.

In the social science realm, Voss et al. (1983) gave a complex, policy-oriented problem to a group of political scientists and chemists. The political scientists (the experts) devoted a large proportion of their problem-solving time to conceptualizing the problem. They formed early tentative hypotheses to guide their exploration of the problem space. Their solutions were fewer and more abstract, and included arguments and explanations. It was clear their knowledge of this type of problem enabled them to recognize patterns, foresee consequences or new problems that might arise, and to discuss the implications of the solutions they examined.

The chemists (considered novices), lacking that familiarity, found it difficult to prioritize the information. They had trouble seeing the big picture and making connections between ideas. Their problem solving process appeared more halting. They typically developed specific, linear, stop-gap solutions (Voss et al., 1983).

In terms of problem solving, the political scientists did a better job. Their representations allowed for greater flexibility in discussing the problem; their solutions covered more possible situations. By looking at their approach to problem solving, we can see that being able to focus on the problem definition and seeing patterns tend to lead to a more effective problem solving effort.

Bardwell (1989) looked at the problem characterizations of college students in an environmental studies course. While none of the students were experts in the topic area (pesticides), the range of problem solving approaches they used approximate those found in the novice/expert research above—linear and patterned.

The linear characterizations reflect the concrete, context-bound connections of map building, similar to those used by a novice. The students relying on this approach

---

[2] In this context, then, experts are not necessarily famous, nor need they wear ties and stiff collars. We all have expertise in something. Interestingly, there are costs to expertise as well. Having a very compact map can blind us to new options and novel ideas. For a fascinating discussion, see Kaplan & Kaplan, 1982.

progressed from start directly to goal, rarely going beyond the information given in the article they read on pesticides. Some of them jumped quickly to a solution, embedding it in their problem definition: "The problem is we need to be better educated." Others would lay out a causal sequence that explained why the problem is a problem and quickly moved to a solution: "This is a problem because...."

The students who presented more patterned characterizations of the problem had richer associative structures and brought in outside information. These approaches reflect a hierarchical understanding and cross-map comparisons, strategies more typical of an expert. Rather than a linear delineation, these students developed a framework within which to look at the problem, and then discussed its various aspects.

The least effective of these patterned approaches involved an emotive assessment of the issue: "It is not fair that farm workers are poisoned by pesticides." Another approach was to use an analogy or describe the problem in terms of another more familiar situation: "This is just like the Romans weakening their whole empire...." The most sophisticated analysis was one in which the student examined the problem from a variety of orientations incorporating political, social, and technological considerations. This presents a richer, more comprehensive problem approach: "The problem is no longer how to deal with insects, but how to deal with farmers' insistence on using these deadly chemicals."

The solutions generated by these approaches also differed. A linear approach works for problems with right and wrong answers. In this instance, as with many environmental issues that require a cross-disciplinary approach, however, a successful solution is more likely to occur in the pattern characterization. Those who remain in the linear mode will not have a rich enough associative structure to fathom the implications which might arise from their proposed solutions.

The question for educators emerging from all of these studies is: how do I help problem solvers use more patterned approaches in their efforts to think about complex, real-world problems? Such an improvement would assist learners with Step 1 of the problem solving process. Is this enough to ensure more facile problem solvers? It is important to recognize that effective problem solving entails using several approaches, and that the approach one chooses does not guarantee a right answer. Nevertheless, we need to encourage students to try a patterned approach, where they explore a problem, move forward and backward or up and down between levels of the problem/solution spaces and struggle with different definitions and solutions. That process will

> make us aware of the options and encourage more thoughtful analysis. Hopefully, it will increase the probability of designing successful solutions and minimize the likelihood of negative outcomes. (Rappaport, 1986, p. 6)

Implications For Teaching Environmental Problem Solving

Cognitive theories of problem solving and information processing help us understand what goes on in our brains as we approach complex problems. In the first step of solving environmental problems, we explore the problem. Because of the nature of environmental problems, this step requires that we consider the issue from several perspectives, applying relevant knowledge from our daily lives and from the scientific, social science, and technological realms. However, this integration is not something people necessarily do of their own accord. Several domains of knowledge are rarely integrated or referred to when people problem solve a multidisciplinary issue (Tudor, 1989; Fleming, 1986; Soloman, 1984). Addressing multi-disciplinary issues requires skills developed through experience, not those automatically generalized from other domains. It is the role of educators to help develop these skills.

In the second step of solving environmental problems, we construct a solution space that allows us to move between the problem and the goal along various paths, checking for a realistic solution, modifying the information, and returning again to match the proposed solution to the goal. Again, such a methodical process does not come naturally to humans. We tend to leap to conclusions, even on limited and uncertain information. To teach problem solving skills, we must help learners develop the ability to manipulate and play with this information. Furthermore, students may need help figuring out how to structure the problem and solution spaces and, at the same time, remain flexible in how they proceed.

In this context, what does it mean to teach problem solving skills? There are three important goals for educators to improve problem solving skills:

1. Familiarity
2. Structure
3. Flexibility

Familiarity: Having Something in One's Head

Familiarity refers to the stuff of problem solving. The term encompasses more than information and facts; it includes learners' familiarity with process and an understanding of their own capabilities. Problem solvers need the following:

Imagery about the problem, possible solutions, and about the problem solving process itself: They need to be familiar not only with the issues, but with possible strategies for solving them, with previous efforts that have succeeded, and some sense of what behaviors or actions are appropriate (Gray, 1985).

In terms of environmental education, the ecological basics are essential to learners' understanding and ability to fit problems into both a historical and biological context. However, equally important is familiarity with the social, political, and cultural aspects of environmental issues. Field trips, computer simulations and role plays, and speakers are commonly used approaches. Success stories (Bardwell, 1991b) offer an efficient in-class mechanism for providing students with imagery of what others have done.

Competence and efficacy. Having some sense of our personal resources and capabilities, and of how they fit with other available resources or levels of action (e.g., in one's community or family) are essential to effective problem solving. While they cannot ensure success, educators can improve the odds by helping learners assess the level at which they choose to address a problem. Alice Steinbach, for example, worked with her students to identify individual projects based on their talents and interest. The Manomet wetlands project (p. 125) encouraged the involvement of an entire community by providing opportunities that required a range of different skills and resources.

Personal commitment. It is hard to solve problems if one does not care. Students need to see how an issue matters to them, or to be able to identify issues that *do* matter. It helps if they have some sense of investment and believe that people just like them solve these problems. Many of the practitioners in Chapter 3 attributed their success to factors that supported students taking responsibility and investing in the issue: the learners chose the problem; the issues were small-scale so that the students could have an impact; and issues involved local concerns students cared about.

As these examples of imagery indicate, simply presenting information is no guarantee that students will become concerned and know how to be problem solvers. Building familiarity requires more; that information needs to tap into the existing maps people have. It is crucial that educators know how their learners think about an issue and invite their participation in the learning process. Although this information is not sufficient, it is an important first step in the problem solving process.

One could begin with the third step in the problem solving process by taking action on a problem that already concerns the students. As students hypothesize about solutions, they will learn more about the ins and outs of the issue. Ideally they will gain some facility in strategizing, working with one another, interacting with others in their community, and actually doing something to address the issue they have defined. Such an approach, however, is not always feasible given constraints teachers face in terms of time, resources, and unsupportive institutional climates.

Other avenues for building familiarity with issues, such as stories, interviews, discussing issues and solutions, and modeling others (Bardwell, 1991b; Vitz, 1990; Monroe & Kaplan, 1988) are more vicarious and flexible. At their best, these approaches deal not only with possible solutions, but explicitly recognize the process so that students can become aware of the skills and strategies as a guide for their problem solving effort (Collins et al., 1991).

The cognitive perspective developed here has stressed that we rely on experience and repeated exposure for building maps and patterns about these issues. This perspective also suggests that students will be better problem solvers if they learn about multiple examples rather than work solely on one action project. They would become familiar with a variety of related but slightly different situations. This, in turn, would facilitate the transferability of their understanding to other situations. It is not surprising that Monroe & Kaplan (1988) found the two most effective approaches for teaching students about environmental problem solving were case studies and talking with others about solutions.

Structure: Staying in the Problem Space

As they rush to collect facts and make decisions, students will need help organizing and managing the information. This will help them separate fact from opinion, and provide the perspective they need to see the issue from different vantages. Structure refers to a meaningful interpretation and organization of this content. How one looks at a problem determines the nature of one's response (Posner, 1973). A psychological perspective that considers cognitive capacity and people's discomfort with confusion suggests some approaches for providing enough structure that students can focus on problem definition (from Bardwell, 1991a):

Limiting information. It is easy to overwhelm people with data and information. Those who insist on fitting in one more fact risk losing others' interest. On the other hand, a problem solving effort that focuses on managing and organizing the relevant information has a fighting chance. Simon notes:

> In a world where information is relatively scarce, and where problems for decision are few and simple, information is almost always a positive good. In a world where attention is a major resource, information may be an expensive luxury, for it may turn our attention from what is important to what is unimportant. We cannot afford to attend to information simply because it is there. (Simon, 1978, p. 13)

Learners, then, need practice in managing the overwhelming amounts of information they encounter every day and in choosing and organizing that which is most relevant and helpful.

Choosing levels. An appropriate level for approaching a problem would be one that fits with one's resources, capabilities, and time. This balance is a delicate one. A problem conceptualized at too global a level can be overwhelming; if defined too specifically, it may seem insignificant and dismissible. Janet Ady's "Teaching about Geese," (p. 123) for example, takes a chunk of the complex, far-reaching issue of species loss. While the curriculum addresses issues of wetlands and population dynamics, it is within the context of four species of geese that play an important role in the community. As her description suggests, the program helped people see that they had profound impacts on the viability of that resource, *and* that they could do something about it.

As in this example, we can have broader-reaching intents, but the focus of our energy is on the doable. Being able to simplify a problem into a manageable number of parts implies that we have an overall sense of how those pieces fit back together. This coherence should enhance our comfort with addressing the problem.

Staying off solutions. Finally, structure can help one stay off solutions. Simple as it sounds, staying with the problem definition and not jumping to conclusions is difficult.

Flexibility: Shifting Levels/Taking Different Vantages

One facet of the expert problem approach was the ability to shift levels and toy with options. Just as familiarity facilitates structure and staying in the problem space, it also means one has room to play with ideas rather than move right into solutions. Flexibility relates to having strategies for managing and dealing with information and seeing it from different perspectives.

One effective strategy mentioned above is to break down a problem into parts (dealing with aspects that are more manageable and about which students have more familiarity) and then put it back together. Again, we can see this strategy in the expert's tendency to move between the different problem levels, and between the problem and solution spaces themselves.

Another strategy entails working backwards from a solution to figure out what kind of problem definition might have spawned it. Working backwards from a "build a nuclear power plant" option, for example, might lead we to a "we need more energy" problem definition. An examination of some underlying assumptions (e.g., that we are effectively using the energy we have) would find that fallacious. A redefinition àla Amory Lovins (1977), "We need to use our energy more efficiently" leads to a different set of options. Case studies, too, provide avenues for exploring what happened and why. Reconstructing history in retrospect helps students think about underlying assumptions and their implications. They can work forward with consecutive pieces of information, or backward from the resolution.

The Educator's Role

These three goals related to familiarity, structure, and flexibility speak to both cognitive and affective factors of problem solving. Learners are going to be emotionally involved in many of these issues. They are going to want answers and solutions because they care. And, there is going to be conflict when they disagree. As they become more familiar with an issue, students will be better able to focus on the problem and stay off solutions. As they practice conflict management and interpersonal skills, they will improve how they address disagreements and manage group process.

A critical role of the educator is to help students develop skills and outlooks that help them manage and guide what is really a struggle for clarity—both cognitively, in terms of their discomfort with uncertainty, *and* affectively, in terms of wanting a solution that quiets their concerns. These skills and outlooks can best be developed in a learning setting that provides enough structure that students have some understanding of and confidence about what they are doing. There need to be explicit, shared expectations and guidelines for group interaction. At the same time, this setting allows enough flexibility that students can choose, explore, fail, and try again.

How might you, as an educator, build a classroom environment that encourages exploration? How can you help students tolerate some of the ambiguity they experience in approaching these problems? Collins et al (1991) would contend, by being a model and facilitator who helps students observe and practice the cognitive and metacognitive skills needed to be better problem solvers. They describe a process, "cognitive apprenticeship" as a mode of instruction that strives to make thinking visible. The teacher's success at "scaffolding," supporting students only as much as needed, allows them to build confidence as they master skills.

These guidelines provide a linkage between the theory of Chapter 1 and the practitioners' applications in Chapter 3:

1. Identify the processes of the task and make them visible to students.

2. Situate abstract tasks in authentic contexts, so students understand the relevance of the work.

3. Vary the diversity of situations and articulate the common elements so students can transfer what they learn.

In such settings, learners have or acquire the requisite knowledge and skills to

1. Collect facts, formulate opinions, and recognize the type of information (whether global or specific) needed.

2. Manage information and set constraints so they are not overwhelmed.

3. Tolerate ambiguity and withhold final conclusions until the problem can be fully examined.

4. Conceptually explore, move back and forth and up and down, through levels of the cognitive hierarchy.

5. Feel competent and experience some sense of success and meaningful participation.

6. Develop the facility to monitor their own problem solving process.

The next two chapters provide some insights into and support for how others have achieved these objectives. All of them echo the themes raised here. Learners need to be able to practice problem solving in a safe setting and to have some imagery of possible strategies and their outcomes. They recognize the need for activities that build skills in group interaction, information and idea sharing, constructive feedback, and valuing others. Finally, they all stress the importance of learners' realizing some kind of success in their efforts. Learners must have an experience they can view positively and see as a part of something larger in a way that matters.

References

Bardwell, L.V. (1989). Managing helplessness and enhancing problem definition in the context of undergraduate environmental instruction. Unpublished dissertation. University of Michigan: Ann Arbor.

Bardwell, L.V. (1991a). Problem-framing: A perspective on environmental problem solving. *Environmental Management* 15(5): 603-612.

Bardwell, L.V. (1991b). Success stories: Imagery by example. *Journal of Environmental Education* 23(1): 5-10.

Collins, A., Brown, J.S., & Holum, A. (1991). Cognitive apprenticeship: Making thinking visible. *American Educator* Winter: 6-46.

UNESCO. (1978, January). The Tbilisi Declaration. *Connect*: UNESCO-UNEP Environmental Education Newsletter 3 (1): 1-8.

Fleming, R.W. (1986). Adolescent reasoning in socio-scientific issues. *Journal of Research in Science Teaching* 23(8): 677-687.

Gagne, E.D. (1985). *The cognitive psychology of school learning.* Boston: Little & Brown.

Gray, D. (1985). *Ecological beliefs and behaviors: Assessment and change.* Westport, CT: Greenwood Press.

Kaplan S. & Kaplan, R. (1982). *Cognition and environment: Functioning in an uncertain world.* New York: Praeger.

Lovins, A. (1977). *Soft energy paths: Toward a durable peace.* Cambridge, MA: Ballinger.

Mandler, G. (1975). Memory storage and retrieval: Some limits on the research of attention and consciousness. In P.M. Rabbitt & S. Dornic (Eds.) *Attention and performance.* (Vol. 5). London: Academic.

Monroe, M.C. & Kaplan, S. (1988). When words speak louder than actions: Environmental problem solving in the classroom. *Journal of Environmental Education* 19(3): 38-41.

Posner, M.I. (1973). *Cognition: An introduction*. Glenview, IL: Scott Foreman.

Rappaport, J. (1986). In praise of paradox: A social policy of empowerment over prevention. In E. Seidman & J. Rappaport (Eds.) *Redefining social problems*. New York: Plenum.

Sanford, A. (1985). *Cognition and cognitive psychology*. New York: Basic Books.

Simon, H. (1978). Rationality as a process and as a product of thought. *American Economic Review* 68: 1-16.

Solomon, J. (1984). Prompts, cues and discrimination: The utilization of two separate knowledge systems. *European Journal of Science Education* 6(3): 277-284.

Tudor, M.T. (1992). Expert and novice differences in strategies to problem solve an environmental issue. *Contemporary Educational Psychology* 17: 329-339.

Vitz, P.C. (1990). The use of stories in moral development: New psychological reasons for an old education method. *American Psychologist* 45(6): 709-720.

Volk, T.L., Hungerford, H.R., & Tomera, A.N. (1984). A national survey of curriculum needs as perceived by professional environmental educators. *Journal of Environmental Education* 16(1):36-40.

Voss, J.F., Tyler, S.W., & Yengo, L.A. (1983). Individual differences in the solving of social science problems. In R.F. Dillon & R.R. Schmeck (Eds.) *Individual differences in psychology*. New York: Academic.

MODELS AND APPROACHES

Introduction

The previous chapter presented a framework for understanding some of the challenges of environmental problem solving. This chapter presents four approaches developed by leading environmental educators for teaching environmental problem solving. In collaboration with several co-authors, Harold Hungerford, William Hammond, William Stapp, and Ian Robottom have submitted descriptions of their approaches, each including reports of how students successfully effected some changes in their communities. Part 5, the final section, provides a brief overview of some of the similarities and differences among the approaches to help teachers fashion their own learning setting for environmental issue problem solving.

MODELS AND APPROACHES : PART 1
Editors' Introduction

Issue Investigation & Citizenship Action Training:
Austin Winther, Trudi Volk, and Harold Hungerford

Winther, Volk, and Hungerford maintain that the process and skills for environmental issue problem solving require specific training. Their research on this teaching model and behavior changes has suggested that citizens are not likely to try to address environmental issues unless they have training on how to investigate and analyze issues and develop plans of action. Under Hungerford's leadership, educators at Southern Illinois University have developed a systematic, scientifically oriented training plan for students to gain problem solving skills. Teachers lead students through several phases of problem solving. In phase one, students learn investigative skills and values analysis techniques. In phase two, they practice these skills in a group investigation of a local issue. During phase three, students create an action plan and become familiar with a range of strategies for taking action. Students are not required to implement their action plan in this program.

What Happens in the Classroom

Teachers use a published manual to lead discussions or assign activities to practice skills of secondary research (using the card catalogue) and primary research (interviewing, collecting data). Eventually, students explore an issue in small groups or as a class, analyzing the various positions and perspectives. Students evaluate alternatives and explore five possible types of action. This process can evolve to real-world action taking, but it need not.

Assumptions about Problem Solving

Problem solving skills depend primarily on understanding the issue. Issue investigation skills are sequential, linear, logical, and transferable from one problem to another. Values positions can be explored and students' positions determined from the evidence. Personal beliefs and values make relevant contributions. New information developed by students is limited by the research questions and available background information.

Learning

This model advocates learning skills in investigation and action taking. Modules provide instruction on action possibilities. Groups and individuals develop action plans and are encouraged, but not required, to carry these out. Problem solving process requires students to develop higher order critical thinking skills.

Teaching Strategies

Structured skill development program is available through curriculum modules developed by Hungerford and others. Teachers primarily use direct instruction for skill development, though cooperative learning is encouraged. Small-group and individual projects are often part of the investigation.

Student Role and Involvement

Specific skills are introduced to, practiced by, and applied by middle school students. Unless the "case study" approach is used, students become familiar with a wide range of issues during the skill development phase and focus on a local issue of their choice during the application phase.

Evaluation Strategies

Students must reach competency in skills before doing an original investigation. Exercises to develop skills are provided. Teacher developed skill tests can be used. Students sign a contract with the teacher on an investigation plan and the teacher evaluates progress on the contract. Sample contracts are provided in modules. Students prepare final oral and written reports on their issues for class presentation and teacher evaluation.

TABLE 2:1
Summary of the
Hungerford et al.
Environmental
Issue Problem
Solving Approach

References

Hines, J.M., Hungerford, H.R., & Tomera, A.N. (1986/7). Analysis and synthesis of research on responsible environmental behavior: A meta-analysis. *Journal of Environmental Education* 18(2):1–8.

Hungerford, H.R., Litherland, R.A., Peyton, R.B., Ramsey, J.M., & Volk, T.L. (1992). *Investigating and evaluating environmental issues and actions: Skill development modules.* Champaign, IL: Stipes Publishing Company.

Hungerford, H.R., Peyton, R.B., & Wilke, R.J. (1980). Goals for curriculum development in environmental education. *Journal of Environmental Education* 1(3):42–47.

Hungerford, H.R., Ramsey, J.M., & Volk, T.L. (1989). What we 'know' about STS citizenship behavior from selected research articles [Unpublished Paper]. Science Education Center, Department of Curriculum and Instruction, Southern Illinois University at Carbondale.

Hungerford, H.R. & Volk, T.L. (1990). Changing learner behavior through environmental education. *Journal of Environmental Education* 21(3):8-21.

Hungerford, H.R., Volk, T.L., & Ramsey, J. M. (1990). *Science-Technology-Society: Investigating and evaluating STS issues and solutions.* Champaign, IL: Stipes Publishing Company.

Ramsey, J.M. & Hungerford, H.R. (1989). The effects of issue investigation and action training on environmental behavior in seventh grade students. *Journal of Environmental Education* 20(4):29–34.

Ramsey, J., Hungerford, H.R., & Tomera, A.N. (1981). The effects of environmental action and environmental case study instruction on the overt environmental behavior of eighth-grade students. *Journal of Environmental Education* 13(1): 24–29.

Sia, A.P., Hungerford, H.R., & Tomera, A.N. (1985/86). Selected predictors of responsible environmental behavior: An analysis. *Journal of Environmental Education* 17(2): 31–40.

ISSUE INVESTIGATION & CITIZENSHIP ACTION TRAINING:
An Instructional Model for Environmental Education

Austin A. Winther
Trudi L. Volk
Harold R. Hungerford

Introduction

In a rural Midwestern community, several junior high students became interested in a local land use issue. The debate centered on the use of a section of state owned land adjacent to a local river. After conducting a county wide survey, these students used their findings to develop a master plan for the use and development of that public land. They submitted and defended the plan at a public hearing sponsored by the state Department of Conservation. Among the farmers, businessmen, bird watchers, recreationists, and others who spoke at the hearing, these students were the only participants who presented a proposal founded on data-based decision making. The master plan that was ultimately adopted was similar to their proposal.

After surveying local residents regarding attitudes toward the recycling of aluminum beverage containers, an eighth grade student in a medium-sized town in central Illinois visited the mayor and shared the results of her issue investigation and survey. The mayor was so impressed with her findings he invited her to address the city council. As a result of her survey and work with the city council, the town now has two recycling centers.

Two secondary students in a large urban area in Missouri noticed the increasing deterioration of their neighborhood. Upon investigating, they discovered a large corporation, after failing at an earlier attempt to rezone the neighborhood for business development, had been quietly buying up residences and allowing them to deteriorate. The students interviewed neighborhood residents, documented the actions of the corporation, and presented their findings to the city council.

Historically, education is responsible for imparting important knowledge and skills. Thus, the schools are responsible for teaching learners to read and write as well as important concepts about the world in which they live. More than that though, schools are supposed to teach learners how to be productive citizens—how to get along with other human beings and what is expected of them in society. Some behaviors are clearly defined and easily measured: knowing how to spell and recalling important facts. Other behaviors, such as being able to obtain gainful employment or developing social skills, are more complex. We also believe responsible citizenship action with respect to the environment is an essential component of education for all of us at the close of the twentieth century. This paper will describe a model of environmental education that has been shown to be effective in shaping such behavior.

If students are to become responsible citizens who understand and act effectively on environmental issues, they should first understand, at least nominally, the scientific principles involved in the issues. They must also understand the positions, beliefs, and values of the people involved in the issues. They should be able to investigate the issues within their community in order to make sound decisions regarding the solution of particular issues. Finally, if they are to play a positive role in the constructive resolution of the issue, they must be able to develop sound action plans, and at the same time, communicate and work with people who hold values and positions different from their own.

Goals of Environmental Education

The model of environmental education we will describe is best understood in terms of goals which have been developed by Hungerford, Peyton, and Wilke (1980). These goals are based on Harvey's work (1977) as well as the Belgrade Charter (1976) and the 1977 Tbilisi Intergovernmental Conference Report (UNESCO, 1978). They include a superordinate goal and four subordinate-level goals.

The Superordinate Goal:

> ... to aid citizens in becoming environmentally knowledgeable and, above all, skilled and dedicated citizens who are willing to work, individually and collectively, toward achieving and/or maintaining a dynamic equilibrium between the quality of life and the quality of the environment (Hungerford, Peyton, & Wilke, 1980, p. 43).

Related to this overall goal for environmental education are four major levels of subgoals which were developed to lead the learner toward the superordinate goal:

Goal Level I: The Ecological Foundations Level

Instruction at this level seeks to provide learners with sufficient ecological knowledge to permit him/her to eventually make ecologically sound decisions with respect to environmental issues.

Goal Level II: The Conceptual Awareness Level

This level of instruction seeks to guide the development of a conceptual awareness of how individual and collective actions may influence the relationship between quality of life and the quality of the environment and, also, how these actions result in environmental issues which may be resolved through investigation, evaluation, values clarification, decision making, and finally citizenship action.

Goal Level III: The Investigation and Evaluation Level

Education at this level provides for the development of the knowledge and skills necessary to permit learners to investigate environmental issues and evaluate alternative solutions for solving these issues. Similarly, values are clarified with respect to issues and alternative solutions.

Goal Level IV: Action Skills Level-Training and Application
Education at this level seeks to guide the development of those
skills necessary for learners to take positive environmental action
for the purpose of achieving and / or maintaining a dynamic equilib-
rium between the quality of life and the quality of the environment
(Hungerford & Volk, 1990, p. 13).

The Instructional Model

To meet these goals a series of curricular materials has been developed. These
curricula have been produced to help students learn how to investigate and evaluate issues and solutions. The authors have used an instructional format where
skills are introduced to the students, practiced by the students, and finally applied
by the students. Transfer of these skills to new and unique situations is expected
and is observed. What follows is a brief description of the instructional sequence
which occurs within the issue investigation and action training instruction.

In the first phase of this approach, students are taught to identify environmental
problems and issues. A problem is any situation in which something valuable is at
risk. An issue arises when two or more parties, called players, disagree about the
solution to a problem. In an environmental problem or issue, some part of the
environment is at risk, but so may be jobs, homes, health, cultural or recreational
resources, or other things of value. Issues may arise when two players have different
knowledge of an issue. However, it is just as likely that two players differ on an
issue because of different beliefs and values.

Students are taught to identify an issue and to analyze it in terms of the issue itself,
the players, their positions, their beliefs, and their values. Value descriptors
(samples of which can be found in Figure 2:1) are provided to help students
identify the values of the players.

To practice these skills, students read and analyze articles related to ongoing
environmental issues from newspapers and magazines. In addition, videotapes
related to issues may be viewed and analyzed. Cooperative learning is encouraged
throughout.

Students are then taught investigation skills so that they can conduct their own
investigations of issues of interest to them which affect their community. These
skills include identifying variables; specifying relationships between variables;
identifying appropriate populations; sampling techniques; questionnaire formulation; and data collection, tabulation, and interpretation. The students practice these
skills individually and in groups.

The next phase of the course involves the original investigation of an issue. The
students are required to identify an issue and conduct a library search of relevant
material. They must identify the players in the issue, as well as their positions,
beliefs, and values.

FIGURE 2:1
Sample Value
Descriptors

Value	Definition
Ecological	pertaining to the maintenance of natural biological systems.
Educational	concerning the accumulation, use, and communication of knowledge; learning about something.
Egocentric	pertaining to a focus on self-centered needs and fulfillments; a "me" value.
Ethical/Moral	pertaining to present and future human responsibilities, rights and wrongs, and standards of conduct.
Legal	relating to national, state, or local laws; law enforcement; lawsuits.
Political	the activities, functions, and policies of governments and their agents.
Religious	the use of belief systems based on faith or dogma.
Social	pertaining to shared human empathy, feelings, and status; a "togetherness" value.

They must determine the scientific validity of the claims of each player. They must also decide, on the basis of the available scientific information and their own values, what their position is on the issue.

The students then formulate research questions. They identify important variables related to the issue they are investigating. The most commonly identified variables include demographic data such as age, gender, and educational level; perceived knowledge about the issue; knowledge of the issue; beliefs about the issue; actions taken with respect to the issue; and intention to act on the issue. Research questions are then formulated using the guidelines given in Figure 2:2. The research questions will guide the investigation and lead to recommendations about the issue and its alternative solutions. Some examples of research questions are given in Figure 2:3.

The students decide on a population to sample and on an appropriate sampling method. These decisions are made on the basis of their research questions. They then develop an instrument to gather the data they will need to answer their research questions. They may gather data through directly observing physical situations or behavior, by asking factual questions concerning behavior or demographics, or by polling concerning opinions and knowledge. Often a combination of these approaches is used.

After the data collection, students tabulate and interpret their findings. This process involves constructing data tables and graphs to understand and report their data. It also includes drawing conclusions and making inferences and recommendations based on their data.

FIGURE 2:2
*Research
Question
Guidelines*

Research Questions:

1. ....are always stated in question form.

2. ....always avoid simple "yes" or "no" responses. Use phrases such as "To what extent" and "In what ways."

3. ....always indicate a population or area.

4. ....are always derived from and related to environmental or other STS issues.

5. ....when possible, specify the variables to be measured.

6. ....when possible, specify a relationship between variables.

7. ....are important scientifically, technologically, or socially.

Note: Research questions should be of genuine interest. They should pertain to "real life." They should be phrased in such a way that they are "answerable" by you and your colleagues.

FIGURE 2:2
*Research
Question
Guidelines*

The final phase, citizenship action, is the formulation of an action plan on the basis of the background research and the survey results. Students are guided to consider individual as well as group actions. They consider four types of actions: persuasion, consumerism, political action, and ecomanagement. A fifth type, legal action, may be briefly discussed. Legal action is usually not emphasized with K-12 students because of the difficulties they might encounter in carrying it out. Descriptions of the four most commonly used methods of action are in Figure 2:4.

FIGURE 2:3
*Sample Research
Questions*

1. To what extent do the citizens of Wayne County believe that a low-level radioactive waste dump should be installed in the county?

2. What are the beliefs and values of Wayne County public officials toward the installation of a low-level radioactive waste dump in the county?

3. To what extent do the farmers of southern Illinois believe that the deer herd is doing significant damage to agricultural crops in the region?

4. In what ways does public sentiment toward the trapping of fur-bearing animals influence coat-buying consumer behavior in suburban Denver?

5. How knowledgeable are the citizens of Phoenix concerning the public health dimensions of air pollution?

6. To what extent do the citizens of Los Angeles believe that water is being wasted by housing and commercial developers? ...by home owners?...by hotels and motels?

FIGURE 2:4
Methods of
Action

Action Method I: Persuasion
Persuasion is used when someone or a group of people try to convince others that a certain action is correct.

Action Method II: Consumerism
Consumerism relies on the power of the pocketbook. It involves buying or not buying something.

Action Method III: Political Action
Political action refers to any mode of action that brings pressure on political or governmental agencies and/or individuals. This includes supporting political candidates, and pressuring people in office through letters, petitions, telegrams, and phone calls.

Action Method IV: Ecomanagement
Ecomanagement is physical action taken with respect to the environment.

In addition to the type of action to take, students decide which level of action—local, state, or national—is most appropriate for their issue. Specific action plans are formulated that reflect the type and level of actions the students decide on. Action plans are formulated and evaluated on the basis of 14 action criteria provided to the student. These criteria are listed in Figure 2:5. Students are encouraged, but not required, to carry out their action plans. A number of students have carried out effective action plans described in Table 2:2.

FIGURE 2:5
Action Analysis
Criteria

Fourteen important questions to ask before proceeding with a citizen action:

1. Is there sufficient evidence to warrant action on this issue?

2. Are there alternative actions available for use? What are they?

3. Is the action chosen the most effective one available?

4. Are there legal consequences of this action? If so, what are they?

5. Will there be social consequences of this action? If so, what are they?

6. Will there be economic consequences of this action? If so, what are they?

7. What are the ecological consequences of this action?

8. Do my personal values support this action?

9. Do I understand the beliefs and values of others involved in this issue?

10. Do I understand the procedures necessary to take this action?

11. Do I have the skills needed to complete this action?

12. Do I have the courage to take this action?

13. Do I have the time needed to complete this action?

14. Do I have all the other resources needed to make this action effective?

As a summative activity students usually present an oral report to their class and prepare a written report on their issue. These reports include background information, the learners' research finding, and an action plan on their issue.

A series of textual materials has been developed to implement the model described. The first of these, *Investigating and Evaluating Environmental Issues and Actions* (Hungerford, Litherland, Peyton, Ramsey, & Volk, 1992), focuses exclusively on environmental issues. *Science-Technology-Society: Investigating and evaluating STS issues and solutions* (Hungerford, Volk, & Ramsey, 1990) deals with the broader spectrum of science-related social issues in general, but still has a strong environmental education component. In addition, several extended case studies have been developed (Ramsey, Hungerford, & Volk, 1989; Culen & Simpson, 1988).

The Research Base

The instructional model just described is meant to address the superordinate goal and subgoals presented earlier. A number of research studies have been conducted addressing several related questions: To what extent does the instruction described lead to responsible environmental citizenship action? What variables seem to be most correlated with such behavior? Which of these variables seem most directly influenced by instruction of this kind? What follows is a brief summary of some of these research findings.

Ramsey conducted a quasi-experimental study of intact eighth grade science classes (Ramsey, Hungerford, & Tomera, 1981). He found that students who used the issue investigation and action training approach surpassed other groups on (1) knowledge of citizenship action, (2) knowledge of categories of action, (3) overt citizenship behavior, and (4) categories of citizenship behavior participated in. In a follow-up to this study, Klinger (1980) found that students who received issue investigation and citizenship action training knew more about citizenship action and took significantly more actions in an effort to resolve issues than students who received only issue investigation training.

Sia sought to identify key variables linked to proenvironmental behavior, and to compare these predictor variables in samples taken from members of an environmental organization and a nonenvironmental organization (Sia, Hungerford, & Tomera, 1985). The eight predictor variables were environmental sensitivity, perceived knowledge of environmental action strategies, perceived skill in using environmental action strategies, psychological sex role classification, individual locus of control, group locus of control, attitude toward pollution, and attitude toward technology. All the predictor variables except attitude toward technology were found to be statistically significantly correlated with overt proenvironmental behavior. Three key variables, perceived skill in using environmental action strategies, level of environmental sensitivity, and perceived knowledge of environmental action strategies, were found to be major predictors of overt responsible environmental behavior.

TABLE 2:2: Citizenship Action Examples

A middle school student in rural western Kentucky became interested in water treatment in her community. After obtaining a water-test-kit from her local water utility she tested her household water supply as well as the local school supply. Alarmed at the abnormally high chlorine content, she contacted community officials. They retested the water and confirmed her findings. She was commended by community officials for her discovery and assured that prolonged exposure to those high rates might have indeed had negative effects on the health of the students.

Two eighth-grade students in down-state Illinois decided to see if bottle bills (legislation supporting a deposit on beverage containers) were workable solutions to roadside littering and the use of a limited resource. They wrote to officials in each of the states with such legislation, and collected information on its effectiveness, administrative costs, and on the perceived positive and negative effects of the legislation. Convinced of the economic and environmental benefits of such legislation, they decided Illinois could benefit from a bottle bill and that bottle bill legislation, currently in committee, should be supported. Garnering the support of their colleagues, and then of citizens in three other area communities, these two students developed a "Bottle Bill Coalition" to lobby lawmakers.

One middle school class in the coalition wrote letters to elected officials. A second invited local representatives to a meeting to discuss their concerns. A third class in another community visited elected officials in the state capitol and lobbied for support of the bill. The two students who spearheaded the coalition convinced their friends to collect aluminum cans, clean them, crush them, and package them in one-pound bundles to mail to the committee members. Each aluminum bundle was accompanied by a petition supporting the proposed legislation. Although Illinois still does not have a bottle bill, that legislative session witnessed the passage of a bill that banned the removable tab considered harmful to humans and animals.

In 1989, an entire class of middle school students in central Wisconsin decided to investigate the proposed timber wolf recovery plan for northern Wisconsin. To do so they developed, with the help of their teacher, a 10-question survey instrument and sent it to 350 randomly selected residents in northern Wisconsin. Amazingly, they obtained a 60% return (211 surveys). Their analysis of the results showed many different attitudes, beliefs, and values regarding wolves and the recovery plan. But, overall, three-fourths of the respondents had a positive attitude toward the plan. To help facilitate the wolf recovery plan, the class chose, as an action plan, to raise money to send to the Timber Wolf Alliance, a group working toward timber wolf recovery in Wisconsin. Using a variety of wolf-related money-making activities, these fifth graders raised $101.00.

Two seventh-grade students in a junior high in the Midwest decided that abandoned vehicles in their community were a real problem. They set about inventorying all abandoned autos in the town. When they completed the neighborhood-by-neighborhood survey, they reported their findings to their class. It was a good and accurate survey with detailed findings. However, what their teacher didn't know was they also reported their findings to the police. One vehicle had been abandoned on a street where they felt everyone would see it. This one, in particular, made them angry. They asked the police to have it moved. The police didn't respond. They asked the police again. Still no results. However, after badgering the police several times, the students succeeded in getting action. This was done without the knowledge of their teacher. When the police called to tell the teacher "his car" had been moved, he thought that his own automobile had been towed away! Much relieved, he found that it wasn't "his car" after all but the one his students had been upset about.

Ramsey conducted a quasi-experimental study which built on his earlier work and the work of Sia (Ramsey & Hungerford, 1989). In it he compared the performance of students who received issue investigation and action training with other students who did not. The dependent variables were overt proenvironmental behavior and several of the variables identified by Sia as being predictors of overt citizenship behavior. He found that the students who received issue investigation and action skill training scored higher than the students who did not on (1) overt citizenship behavior, (2) both individual and group locus of control, (3) knowledge of citizenship action strategies, and (4) perceived skill in the use of citizenship action strategies. The students who received the training in this study had several different teachers and were from different geographic areas. This lends credence to the argument that change in student behavior, as a result of instruction, is possible in a variety of classrooms in diverse geographic locations.

Models of Behavior Change

Traditional thinking in environmental education is that we can change behavior by giving people knowledge about the environment. The reasoning is that by increasing their environmental knowledge we make people more aware of the issues and this awareness changes their attitude. Their newfound positive attitude, in turn, will change the way they behave. This model is represented by Figure 2:6.

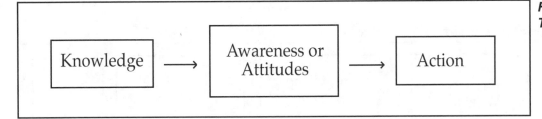

FIGURE 2:6
Traditional Model

Unfortunately, research does not seem to support that model. A number of researchers, in addition to those already cited, have contributed to our understanding of behavior change: Hines, Hungerford, & Tomera, 1986; Borden, 1984-85; Borden & Powell, 1983; Holt, 1988; Koslowsky, Kluger, & Yinon, 1988; Marcinkowski, 1989; Simpson, 1989; Sivek, 1989. There seem to be three levels of variables which contribute to behavior: entry-level variables, ownership variables, and empowerment variables. These three levels are hypothesized to act in more or less linear fashion, albeit a complex one (Hungerford & Volk, 1990). These variables are represented in a flowchart in Figure 2:7.

Entry-level variables are highly correlated to behavior. They may, to some extent, be regarded as prerequisites to proenvironmental behavior. These variables seem least susceptible to short-term instruction. Although they must be present to some extent before proenvironmental behavior is likely to occur, they are not sufficient to ensure positive behavior. These variables, explained below, include environmental sensitivity, androgyny (in the psychological sense); knowledge of ecology; and attitudes towards pollution, technology, and economics.

Environmental sensitivity is defined as an empathetic perspective toward the environment. It is the most important of the entry-level variables and deserves major attention from educators. Androgyny refers to individuals who tend to reflect nontraditional sex-role characteristics. Knowledge of ecology refers to the conceptual framework necessary for sound decision making. It is almost always a prerequisite to decision making. Attitudes toward pollution, technology, and economics have been significant in some studies. They are included as minor variables (Hungerford & Volk, 1990, pp. 11–12).

In addition to the entry-level variables, individuals must possess a sense of both ownership and empowerment before they are likely to take significant actions with regard to the environment (Hungerford, Ramsey, & Volk, 1989). Ownership variables are those that make issues personal for students. The most important of these appear to be in-depth knowledge of issues and personal investment in an issue. In-depth knowledge of issues includes understanding the issue and the human and ecological consequences of the proposed outcomes. Personal investment involves strong personal identification with the issue (Hungerford & Volk, 1990, p. 12).

Important empowerment variables include perceived skill in using environmental action strategies, knowledge of environmental action strategies, locus of control, and intention to act. Perceived skill in environmental action strategies means the learners believe they know how to use a variety of alternative means to influence an issue positively.

FIGURE 2:7 Behavior Flow Chart

	Entry-Level Variables	Ownership Variables	Empowerment Variables	C i t i z e n s h i p
Major Variables	•Environmental sensitivity	• In-depth knowledge about issues	•Knowledge/skill in action strategies •Locus of control • Intention to act	
Minor Variables	• Knowledge of ecology • Androgyny • Attitudes towards pollution, technology, & economics	• Knowledge of consequences • Personal commitment	• In-depth knowledge about issues	B e h a v i o r

Knowledge of environmental action strategies refers to objective understanding of various strategies. The extent to which it is a separate variable from perceived skill in the strategies is not known.

Locus of control refers to the extent to which a person feels he or she can act effectively in a situation. A person with a highly "internal locus of control" feels that he or she can strongly influence the outcome of a situation. A person with highly "external locus of control" feels the outcome of events is largely outside his or her control. People with internal locus of control are more likely to take action than persons with external locus of control. Although locus of control probably cannot be taught, research indicates internal locus of control can be improved by teaching citizenship action strategies. Intention to act appears to be closely related to perceived skill in taking action, locus of control, and personal investment (Hungerford & Volk, 1990, pp.12–13).

The issue investigation and citizenship action training model of environmental education directly addresses several of the variables identified as contributing to proenvironmental behavior. These include in-depth knowledge about issues, personal investment in issues and the environment, knowledge of consequences of behavior, and knowledge and skill in using environmental action strategies. The fact that this model addresses these variables accounts, in part, for the success the model has demonstrated in changing student behavior.

At the same time, however, there are important contributing factors to environmental behavior that this model cannot address. Environmental sensitivity is a key element. Environmental sensitivity seems to be a stable characteristic. Studies by Tanner (1980), Peterson (1982), Scholl-Wilder (1983), and Peters-Grant (1987) seem to indicate this is a result of a wide variety of influences over a long period of time, including early childhood outdoor experiences and role models. Thus, it seems unlikely a one-semester course would have a large impact on it. We don't know what the effects on sensitivity might be if the model we are describing permeated students' schooling.

The work of Sia (1985/86) identified key variables that appear to contribute to responsible environmental behavior, and Marcinkowski (1989) expanded on this work. Progress has been made over the last two decades in understanding and shaping learner behavior in environmental education. Unfortunately, the tasks facing humanity, with respect to the environment, are both enormous and urgent. If we, as environmental educators, are to meet these tasks we must do more and better research. We must do a far better job of translating existing research into practical instructional programs, and we must utilize these programs in a variety of educational settings. The issue investigation and action training model appears to be one step in the right direction.

References

Belgrade Charter. (1976). Connect. *UNESCO-UNEP Environmental Education Newsletter* 1(1): 1–2.

Borden, R. (1984-85). Psychology and ecology: Beliefs in technology and the diffusion of ecological responsibility. *Journal of Environmental Education* 16(2): 14–19.

Borden, R. & Powell, P. (1983). Androgyny and environmental orientation: Individual difference and common commitment. In A. Sacks et al. (Eds.) *Current issues in environmental education and environmental studies*, Vol. 8: 261–275. Columbus, OH: ERIC/SMEAC.

Culen, J. & Simpson, P. (1988). Canada Geese: A wildlife management case study (H.R. Hungerford, J. Ramsey, & T. Volk, Collaborators) Carbondale, IL: Department of Curriculum and Instruction, Southern Illinois University.

Harvey, G.D. (1977). Environmental education: A delineation of substantive structure. *Dissertation Abstracts International* 38, 611A–612A.

Hines, J.M., Hungerford, H.R., & Tomera, A.N. (1986/7). Analysis and synthesis of research on responsible environmental behavior: A meta-analysis. *Journal of Environmental Education* 18(2): 1–8.

Holt, J.G. (1988). A study of the effects of issue investigation and action training on characteristics associated with environmental behavior in non-gifted eighth grade students [Unpublished Research Paper]. Southern Illinois University at Carbondale.

Hungerford, H.R., Litherland, R.A., Peyton, R.B., Ramsey, J.M., & Volk, T.L. (1992). *Investigating and evaluating environmental issues and actions: Skill development modules.* Champaign, IL: Stipes Publishing Company.

Hungerford, H.R., Peyton, R.B., & Wilke, R.J. (1980). Goals for curriculum development in environmental education. *Journal of Environmental Education* 11(3): 42-47.

Hungerford, H.R., Ramsey, J.M., & Volk, T.L. (1989). What we 'know' about STS citizenship behavior from selected research articles [Unpublished Paper]. Science Education Center, Department of Curriculum and Instruction, Southern Illinois University at Carbondale.

Hungerford, H.R. & Volk, T.L. (1990). Changing learner behavior through environmental education. *Journal of Environmental Education* 21(3): 8–21.

Hungerford, H.R., Volk, T.L., & Ramsey, J.M. (1990). *Science-Technology-Society: Investigating and evaluating STS issues and solutions.* Champaign, IL: Stipes Publishing Company.

Klinger, G. (1980). The effect of instructional sequence on the environmental action skills of a sample of southern Illinois eighth graders [Unpublished Research Paper]. Carbondale, IL.

Koslowsky, M.A., Kluger, A.N., & Yinon Y. (1988). Predicting behavior: Combining intention with investment. *Journal of Applied Psychology* 73(1): 102–106.

Marcinkowski, T.J. (1989). An analysis of correlates and predictors of responsible environmental behavior. *Dissertation Abstracts International* 49(12), 3677-A.

Peters-Grant, V.M. (1987). The influence of life experiences in the vocational interests of volunteer environmental workers. *Dissertation Abstracts International* 47, 3744A–3745A.

Peterson, N.J. (1982). Developmental variables affecting environmental sensitivity in professional environmental educators [Unpublished Master's Thesis]. Carbondale, IL: Southern Illinois University at Carbondale.

Ramsey, J.M. & Hungerford, H.R. (1989, Spring). The effects of issue investigation and action training on environmental behavior in seventh grade students. *Journal of Environmental Education* 20(4): 29–34 .

Ramsey J.M., Hungerford, H.R., & Volk, T.L. (1989). A science-technology-society case study: Municipal solid waste. Champaign, Il: Stipes Publishing Company.

Ramsey, J., Hungerford, H.R., & Tomera, A.N. (1981). The effects of environmental action and environmental case study instruction on the overt environmental behavior of eighth-grade students. *Journal of Environmental Education* 13(1): 24–29.

Scholl-Wilder, M. (1983). Significant childhood environmental learning experiences of suburban/urban environmentalists. In J.H. Baldwin (Ed.) *Crossroads: Society and technology*. Proceedings of the 12th Annual Conference of the National Association for Environmental Education. Troy, OH: NAAEE. 125–130.

Sia, A.P., Hungerford, H.R., & Tomera, A.N. (1985/86, Winter). Selected predictors of responsible environmental behavior: An analysis. *Journal of Environmental Education* 17(2): 31–40.

Simpson, P.R. (1989). The effects of an extended case study on citizenship behavior and associated variables in fifth and sixth grade students [Unpublished Doctoral Dissertation]. Southern Illinois University at Carbondale.

Sivek, D. (1989). An analysis of selected predictors of environmental behavior of three conservation organizations. *Dissertation Abstracts International* 49 (11), 3322A.

Tanner, T. (1980). Significant life experiences: A new research area in environmental education. *Journal of Environmental Education* 11 (4): 20–24.

UNESCO. (1978, January). The Tbilisi declaration. *Connect*, UNESCO-UNEP Environmental Education Newsletter, 3 (1): 1–8.

MODELS AND APPROACHES : PART 2

EDITORS' INTRODUCTION

Action Within Schools: William Hammond

Hammond selects students for his program by identifying both the positive and negative leaders of a secondary school class. These leaders are eligible for an independent study class one full day every week over a period of a year. This group embarks on a residential camping experience to build a sense of joint responsibility. Hammond's goal is to build personal and political skills through practical experience addressing significant community issues. He refers to developing skills such as lobbying, analyzing values and points of view, and effective political advocacy. Initially the class selects a community issue which involves elected leaders, and forms groups to handle designated tasks. Hammond has rules the participants must follow as they complete projects. Table 2:3 summarizes Hammond's approach. A discussion of his methodology and experience in environmental issue problem solving follows.

Reference

Hammond, W.F. (1993). *Acting on action as an integral component of schooling.* Ft. Myers, FL: Natural Context.

What Happens in the Classroom

Once a week this group of students meets to build rapport; learn about environmental resources and issues; practice skills in interviewing, lobbying, resolving conflict, and communicating effectively; and collect data. The class members design a plan to contribute to or resolve an issue of their choice that involves elected leaders and community action.

Assumptions About Problem Solving

Students are leaders and their leadership qualities can be improved by offering training, skill building, support, and success. Students must be encouraged to face disappointments with renewed energy, to come back again and again with a different strategy. Success occurs with effort. Environmental issues often involve a political power base, hence the involvement with elected officials.

Learning

Skills are developed or practiced during the process of group problem solving. These skills may be separately developed through direct instruction and constantly reinforced through mentorship and coaching from the teacher. Cooperative, group development is a key component of the educational goals.

Teaching Strategies

The teacher is the coach or mentor. He or she uses direct instruction for significant skills such as lobbying or interviewing, and facilitates the problem solving process and perhaps, the choice of issue. The teacher asks students to envision a solution, and brainstorm alternative actions and realistic expectations.

Student Role and Involvement

Secondary students carry a significant degree of responsibility for creating positive change, by building a group relationship of mutual responsibility, learning about the community resources and issues, choosing their own issue for class investigation, and organizing into action groups. Students plan what will be done each class session. Elementary students may participate by working with the secondary students.

Evaluation Strategies

The project outcome is one element of the evaluation, and the project will continue until there is a positive outcome. Each student is required to invest a certain number of hours. The class sets criteria for grading, and grades are given through mutual consensus of instructor and student. Journals are used for reflection and evaluation.

TABLE 2:3
Summary of the Hammond Environmental Issue Problem Solving Approach

ACTION WITHIN SCHOOLS

WILLIAM F. HAMMOND

Introduction

To gain a perspective on a program for problem solving through the case study model, I believe it is essential to understand the conditions that provided the social, political, educational, and economic context as well as a perspective of the individuals who shaped the formation of this program.

In retrospect, my early educational experiences had a profound effect on the evolution of an environmental issue problem solving approach which became known as the Monday Group Program. My educational outlook was shaped by my experience of growing up in rural New York City where I attended elementary school P.S. #8.

The effect of living in truly rural suburbia, wandering the woods, fields, bays, beaches, and marshes but able to "jump" into one of the world's largest urban centers—New York City—in less than an hour via mass transit provided a broad perspective of my environment. At P.S. #8 , the Deweyian education philosophy was practiced advocating that education is rooted in research, action, and products. This became my model of what teaching and learning ought to be. Participation from elementary through high school in scouting and student government reinforced the sense of importance and the basic responsibility every person has to be a contributing leader in whatever he or she does. Higher education reinforced the importance of field-based instruction, biological-ecological research, and participatory leadership in shaping an environmentally literate person. The seeds for an instructional program developing environmental issue problem solving competence were planted during those years.

After teaching in rural upstate New York for 2 years, a change in family health required a move to Florida in 1961. Lee County, a coastal marine-estuarine dominated environment, had no instructional program connection to the productive environment full of unique critters, flora, and relationships. In addition to adding marine instructional experiences to general science 7 through 9 and biology courses, I started a 6-week marine field and lab program for students grades 7-10. The summer marine course culminating with a week-long snorkeling study trip to the Florida Keys was a big success. We started an evening adult education program in marine biology, and over a 4-year period more than 60% of the physicians in Lee County along with their spouses took the course.

In 1963 we converted a school bus into a mobile field lab. The bus was fully equipped with a lab that supported 10 basic chemical water quality analysis tests using standard methods of the day. It carried 35 microscopes, built-in observation aquaria, saltwater transport barrels, a full complement of net racks, and other equipment. The bus had built-in scuppers for easy hose-out and wash-down, and fold-down work tables facilitated group work on stations. Space was available to transport 40 high school students. The mobile lab bus provided high visibility and served as a platform for teacher training. It enabled students to conduct water quality surveys, tidal flow and current studies, marine flora and fauna studies, beach profile, and related longshore transport studies.

In 1967 the new Cypress Lake High School opened in the district. I created an extensive marine science education program offering three levels of marine science. This unique program changed my teaching direction. It included three students who had published in refereed scientific journals by the time they were eleventh graders. Another student while working at the Duke marine lab in the summer actually collected three previously undescribed plankton species and provided the scientific designation for the species. That first class of 23 students, twelve with I.Q. scores above 120, twelve with scores below 90, and one emotionally troubled student with a score of 100, changed the focus of the school district program from the limited marine biology approach to one that looked at the total environment. This experience reshaped my philosophy of teaching in high school into an action-research, cooperative learning approach.

While I was teaching at Lee Junior High School, two years before going to Cypress Lake, my students initiated a series of Ecology Clubs at all six junior high schools and five high schools. These students conducted monthly meetings with representatives from each club to share successes and plans for future initiatives. When students could not find a recycling outlet for used aluminum, they, with the assistance of Mr. Al Howard, the industrial arts supervisor, got each school's industrial arts department to purchase a small aluminum smelter so the schools could set up their own recycling program. Students brought in aluminum cans for melt down and were given reclaimed aluminum to complete projects. Typical examples of the projects included three cans providing the aluminum to cast a Peace Medallion and two six packs providing the aluminum to cast a model airplane engine block.

The experience provided staff with insight to working with highly motivated students, many not academically successful, but environmentally concerned. The student Ecology Clubs primarily were after school and did not have official support of the school system. In each school I worked with students to recruit teachers to serve as advisors. In 1968, students planned and implemented a cleanup of the roadside canal and ditches along U.S. Highway 41. More than 1,000 students participated in the effort, which included a rally featuring environmental speeches. The student leaders planned and conducted this and all related projects during the "edge of school" meetings in homes and in parks. This situation placed teachers in an awkward and risky position because they worked in a mentoring, facilitating role without pay and only had tacit approval from the school administration. I made my home available to student leaders as a meeting location. This kept me in touch with their thinking.

After the cleanup and rally, student leaders held a follow-up meeting. Here they decided their next project would be to hang two county commissioners in effigy in the old oak tree in front of the county courthouse. When questioned, the students revealed they knew little about the men, their motivations or environmental positions. I realized these highly motivated, environmentally informed students did not have the political skills or tools to work within the democratic system. This led to the formalization of what has become known as the "Monday Groups," action-focused instructional experiences for students of all ages within the context of schooling.

The Monday Group Program

The Monday Group Program is organized by enlisting current and potential high school leaders to attend an environmental education seminar class. This group includes both positive and negative leaders, ranging from mainstream to radical. This broad selection of students has gained support from the principals who endorse the program.

The Monday Group meets a full day, weekly, traditionally on a Monday, and students earn one academic credit for the full-year course. Originally students were required to undertake individual study projects, typically involving their preferred mode of expression (e.g., poetry, music, research reports, etc.). However this requirement has become a minor component to the required input on a class project. The whole class must select a community issue involving elected leaders and design a plan to resolve or contribute to the resolution of the issue within a school year. The initial rationale for working in groups on community problems was to have students learn organizational and leadership skills in a framework involving rights and responsibilities. This rationale grew into the understanding and theoretical assumption that learners forming a community become committed and therefore empowered to solve environmental issues. This process provides the opportunity for students to transfer academic learning through direct community-based applications.

The Monday Group process gets under way by exposing the class to a range of local environmental resources and issues. Students get a chance to wade through wetlands, walk beaches and forests, and inspect local sewage and utility plants. They immerse themselves in their community, reflecting on what is at stake for themselves and future generations.

In order to create optimal group cohesion, the Monday Group typically goes on a residential camping trip during the first month of classes. Students form a tightly knit community while working on personal growth. They experience outdoor activities along with values analysis, conflict resolution, and other kinds of interactive skill building. Leaders from around the state visit the camp to discuss local environmental issues. This initial experience develops a sense of community. Proof of this community is in the consensus the class arrives at in choosing a community problem for a year of focused problem solving attention.

It is important for students to find a project that can be broken down into increments, where a portion may be addressed within the year time frame. The teacher's role often becomes helping students work out a "phase" planning approach. However if the issue is not resolved in the time frame set, the Monday Group is to persist and revisit the problem, reflecting on what can be learned and improved upon from past problem solving attempts. Legacies of previous classes may be analyzed for ideas by the next class. Students attending the Monday Group seminar for more than one year have an opportunity to revisit and recycle the issue. If they wish, they may lobby the new class to continue with the next phase of the project.

The Monday Group seminar class uses as its core curriculum the understanding of "natural models; the principles of diversity, change, interdependence, and the interrelationships of all things and the self-regulating characteristic of natural systems on the planet" (Project WILD, 1992). While the concepts of natural systems are being addressed, skills to become an effective community member, leader, and an independent agent for change are overlain. Teachers and community mentors facilitate skill development of the "action research" process, political efficacy, and research methodology.

Mentoring is key to developing a sense of community commitment. By personally meeting key community players involved in an issue and actively collecting data and practicing "action skills," students build a sense of personal connection to the problem being worked on, which makes the student investigator a stakeholder in the outcome. From community commitment, and knowledge and skills mastered emerges empowerment.

Through the Monday Group the teacher can facilitate specific skill development important in participatory democracy. Students focus on leadership within a group where a leader is any person taking action to move the group toward achieving its goal. Conflict resolution strategies are practiced. Techniques to lobby and use mass media are exercised. Personal skill development through journal keeping is stressed. "Journalling" becomes a method which "balances active expression with relaxed reflection" and becomes a tool to "nurture the growth of personal creativity and connectedness" (Natural Context).

The Monday Group process winds up the year by publicly celebrating the problem solving and actions of the year. The high visibility of the Monday Group serves to validate the action concept as a valued part of the school district's curriculum and belief system. Results and success stories are widely circulated. Successful teachers become peer trainers and gain the support of the administration.

A teacher's role must change from that of a conveyer of information to a teacher-facilitator of action skill development and coach-mentor in the student decision making and implementation of proposed solution processes. One of the most critical teacher roles in implementing action program activities is to coach students in examining and planning. Students need to learn how to break their end goal vision into a subset of enabling or key steps and milestones or critical subgoal accomplishments. If the time constraints of the school setting or political process (which always seems to take longer than estimated) prolong the attainment of the full goal, students will still have a positive sense of accomplishment. They will feel they made a difference and can continue to make a difference if they persist. Other important generic guidelines that have evolved over years of studying successful practices for carrying out action projects or programs in schools are:

1. The learners (not the teacher or other adult) should and select the problem to research and address.

2. A basic set of "action skills" must be taught and applied including how to
    a. identify, research, and investigate the problem or issue selected
    b. be a leader and organize groups
    c. communicate effectively (e.g., letter writing, phone calling, public speaking, lobbying, using the mass media)
    d. present effectively
    e. manage conflicts
    f. determine support and opposition to the solution, select appropriate methods, strategies, and tactics for implementing action using Force Field Analysis
    g. understand alternative strategies and develop capacity for project sustainability and continuity.

In addition, if the project is carried out as a group project it is important the learner master a variety of group collaborative team skills.

The students and teachers also have access to a compilation of Action Skills Modules. The skills modules are designed to complement *Investigating and Evaluating Environmental Issues and Actions Skill Development Modules* (Hungerford, Volk et al., 1992), *Education in Action* (Bull, 1988) and *How Nature Works* (Cohen, 1988) with minimal duplication.

A useful and powerful set of guidelines for the operation of an action program component are found in the *Monday Group Class Guidelines* (or Commandments) below:

*   **Take only positive positions.** If you are opposed to something you must be for something. Therefore it is your responsibility to state your own stand and your proposed solution.

*   **Avoid stereotyping.** Treat everyone as a person of high moral worth. Stereotype labeling (he's a developer, she's an environmentalist, she's a liberal, he's a conservative, etc.) tends to get in the way of establishing positive relationships and communications. Stereotypes are generalizations that limit our ability to communicate with each person for their own knowledge, skills, and unique personality.

- **Do your homework.** Become an expert on your topic. Read articles about your topic, interview experts, do field investigations. Identify the core problem or issue(s) and formulate your research questions and hypothesis to best address the problem and related circumstances.

- **Follow the force field**. Investigate the viewpoints of all stakeholders impacted by the problem or issue, then formulate an action plan, select the strategies and tactics most appropriate to the situation.

- **Avoid scapegoating.** If you fail to attain your goal avoid the temptation to blame your lack of success on someone else or on a set of circumstances. If you failed to attain your desired goal it is because you did not do something(s) you needed to do. The solution is simple ... *RECYCLE.*

- **Recycle.** If you do not reach your intended goal start the process over again. The second or third time you know far more than when you started. You know key resource people, what worked and what did not. Try again and again until you succeed.

- **Be persistent.** Stick with it! Few people expect students to accomplish anything of real substance on environmental problems and issues in their community. Long-term planning, commitment, and a tenacious approach are critical components needed to carry out significant environmental action projects. The action process tends to be a spiraling pattern of action—research—action—research (informed critique)—action. This is where the recycling element is so critical to success, as are support and supportive intervention by mentors.

In an effort to resolve an issue through problem solving there are three levels of action possible to complete the problem solving process. Most initial action projects are at Level 1, be they kindergarten or Grade 12 projects.

Level 1: Carrying out actions that result primarily in an end product

These may include both long-term and short-term projects. Long-term projects: wildlife habitat improvement projects, marking watershed stormwater drainages, developing publications and multimedia programs to inform people on a chosen issue or problem. One-shot projects: planting trees, recycling, building and placing bird or bat boxes in critical locations. Other activities such as writing letters, making phone calls to decision makers, purchasing rainforest acreage all fall into this category. Again, the primary project outcome is to get something done within a given period of time and then move on to another project. The outcome is distinguished by an end product or completion of the project within a school year or possibly longer.

Level 2: Carrying out actions that result in ongoing environmental processes

These actions do not so much accomplish an outcome, but rather are processes that are *sustained in operation in some form of multiyear perpetuity.* This category requires all the requisite skills for a Level 1 project, plus it requires participants to exhibit organizational skills to design and implement a system to sustain the project as an ongoing endeavor after they have moved on.

Level 3: Carrying out actions that result in some level of policy change

This requires the most complex set of skills. It is directed at changing or creating a new public policy at the school, school district, city, county, state, or federal level. Students engaged in this endeavor need all the skills necessary in the other level projects plus sophisticated skills in lobbying, mass media governmental processes, and positive efficacy within the democratic system.

While the levels require different sets of skills, one level is no less or more important than another. There are examples of elementary, middle, and high school students successfully carrying out projects at all levels. The typical pattern for a teacher and students evolves through the levels as skills are acquired and mature. However, some students and teachers have accomplished a Level 3 project without ever completing a Level 1 or 2 project. Motivation, commitment, and skill development are the keys to success.

Why Problem Solving and Action in Education?

In the 1960's environmental education was defined to include three critical components:

1. Developing **awareness** of the environment and one's connections to it,

2. Developing an **understanding** of environmental concepts and knowledge of ecological scientific, social, political and economic systems and,

3. The capacity to **act** responsibly within the processes of our democratic system.

The strategy is based on the premise that an educated person is more likely to be an independent thinker capable of deriving his or her own rational decisions and an active participant in the democratic system. The approach is central to providing students with the opportunity to utilize information and knowledge by transfer to new situations and contexts and thereby demonstrate their understanding of concepts.

A cause for concern is the statistics from the 1980s into the early 1990s which indicate that less than 25% of the citizens of the United States of America under the age of 25 registered to vote. Obviously, something is happening in our society and schools. Despite teaching about government and civic responsibility, students do not feel connected enough to the democratic process to want to participate in the change process in America.

This does not have to be the case. A wide variety of successful instructional programs have been designed and implemented since the early 1960's. These programs clearly demonstrate that if students are taught basic action skills, are actively engaged in playing a positive role in solving local, state, national, and international problems, they will act within the democratic system as responsible citizens while in school and after they graduate. We have many examples of successful student action projects conducted by students from K-12. This expectation is a part of the Lee County school system written curriculum.

Problem Solving and Action within the School Context

Implementing an action component in the context of schooling is different than implementing an action program within community organizations, businesses, special interest groups, and other civic contexts. The schools are obligated not to propagandize and make students self-serving advocates. School personnel have an obligation to provide students with access to a range of viewpoints on potential solutions to values issues. It is important that students recognize that people of good intentions may perceive a problem and its solution differently. It is the responsibility of the educated person, "the students," to make informed decisions about the viewpoints with which they align themselves. If a student is not comfortable (without threat of penalty of any sort) taking a position in opposition to that which the teacher holds, education becomes a program of propaganda and indoctrination.

Key Elements of an Action Program Component in Schools

The Action Element of a sound educational program requires that a student master the basic skills in reading, writing, math, science, social studies, the arts, ecological systems, and technology applications. This in turn provides a powerful life-based context for the direct application of these academics in "the real world." The Action Element brings life to learning since the outcomes are unknown. The experience becomes a problem solving process, providing an opportunity for each learner to bring together what has been learned in school and apply it to the selected problem or issue. The process enhances the development of character skills for students of all ages. Honesty, integrity, work ethic, trust, positive risk taking, collaborative participation, and empathy for others are but a few of the character skills emphasized in action work.

The three important outcomes that are acquired by every student participating in an effective action-based school program are that students tend to become bonded to:

1. **Natural systems** through direct experience and expanded knowledge about how nature works.

2. **Democracy** through personal empowerment and expanded sense of locus of control.

3. **Their community** by developing a "sense of place" or connectedness to a physical place and cultural context.

Conclusion

People choose to act not from a cerebral or pure rational stimulus but from an emotional stimulus. They act because they feel, value, and believe. The available information and data reinforces those emotional stimuli to action and may shape the approach to action. This is why it is so important that firsthand contextual experience be a link in empowering people to action.

The difficulty is where to begin with inexperienced teachers and students to implement action projects within the boundaries of a democratic system. Environmental education programs using the Monday Group approach provide a rich opportunity for practicing critical thinking skills in context while acting on community problems of worth.

References

Bull, J., Cromwell, M., Cwikiel, W., DiChiro, G., Guarino, J., Rathje, R., Stapp, W., Wals, A.E., & Youngquist, M. (1988). *Education in action: A community problem-solving program for schools.* Dexter, MI: Thompson Shore.

Cohen, M.J. (1988). *How nature works.* Walpole, NH: Stillpoint.

Cohen, M.J. (1989). *Connecting with nature.* Eugene, OR: World Peace University.

Hammond, W.F. (1993). *Acting on action as an integral component of schooling.* Ft. Myers, FL: Natural Context.

Hungerford, H.R., Litherland, R.A., Peyton, R.B., Ramsey, J.M., & Volk, T.L. (1992). *Investigating and evaluating environmental issues and actions: Skill development modules: A curriculum development project designed to teach students how to investigate and evaluate science-related social issues.* Champaign, IL: Stipes Publishing Company.

Knapp, C.E. (1992). *Lasting lessons. A teacher's guide to reflecting on experience.* Charleston, WV: ERIC Appalachia Educational Lab.

Lewis, B.A. (1991). *The kid's guide to social action.* Minneapolis: Free Spirit Publishing.

Mitchell, M.K. & Stapp, W.B. (1991). *Field manual for water quality monitoring.* Dexter MI: Thomson-Shore.

Project WILD. (1992). *Project WILD elementary activity guide and secondary activity guides.* Western Regional Environmental Education Council, Project WILD.

MODELS AND APPROACHES : PART 3

Editors' Introduction

An Action Research Approach to Environmental Problem Solving: William Stapp & Arjen Wals

The Action Research Community Problem Solving approach is based on the belief that students should play a role in planning their educational activities. They should have the opportunity to take responsible action. Through that effort, students learn about the problem, the action, and the process of problem solving. The process of researching an issue to come to a problem definition is considered an action and therefore referred to as "action research." Stapp and Wals maintain participants do not have to understand the problem thoroughly before implementing the plan of action, as long as there are opportunities in the plan to assess the outcome and make necessary changes. They refer to this problem solving process as the planning–observing–action–reflection spiral, which is repeated to produce new understanding and improved results. The goal is for students to alleviate the situation, not necessarily resolve it. The Action Research Community Problem Solving process allows teachers to integrate structured and unstructured approaches in community problem solving. The next section begins with Table 2:4, which summarizes the Stapp and Wals approach. Stapp and Wals then discuss the rationale and techniques for engaging in this type of problem solving process.

Reference

Wals, A. & Stapp, W.B. (1989). Education in action: A community problem solving program for schools. In Iozzi, L.A. and Shepard, C.L. (Eds.) *Building multicultural webs through environmental education*. Troy, OH: NAAEE.

TABLE 2:4
Summary of
Stapp & Wals
Environmental
Issue Problem-
Solving Approach

What Happens in the Classroom

Students begin by touring the school and neighborhood to select a problem they wish to impact. They research the topic, set problem objectives, and analyze the problem (who is affected, what created the problem, what is your power, how can it be used?) in small, cooperative groups. They use brain-storming techniques to determine alternate actions and define criteria for the project. They design an action plan and take action. Reflection on the success of their action leads them to revise original plans and repeat the process of plan–observe–act–reflect.

Assumptions about Problem Solving

Environmental issues have societal and environmental aspects and must be understood from both perspectives. A "full" investigation cannot occur before students begin to take action—the process of action and reflection yields additional information that enlarges the understanding of the problem. Students have the capacity to understand and take action; building their confidence and competence is a part of good education.

Learning

Skill building can occur prior to or during the process of problem solving. Teachers should assess student needs to determine if time must be set aside to deliberately build skills. Some skills will be acquired only during the process of problem solving. Emphasis is on group processing, communication, and leadership skills. Many forms of action are possible, including investigating an issue. The repetition of the plan–observe–act–reflect spiral allows students to discover other perspectives of the problem. This is an opportunity to "stay off solutions" and return to earlier phases of problem solving activity.

Teaching Strategies

The teacher is the facilitator of the process (not a commentator or director), a source of information, a coordinator of group activities and field trips. The teacher keeps a journal and log of activities. Team teaching is encouraged to provide additional and interdisciplinary perspectives and divergent views.

Students' Role and Involvement

Students develop confidence in their own abilities to speak, contribute to a group, and analyze information. Students grow with the realization that their interests are more important than the textbook or the teacher's. An entire class may be involved, with small groups working on different aspects of a problem, from several weeks to a semester.

Evaluation Strategies

Student reflection and self-assessment of growth are used, as well as an evaluation of the success of the action, teacher and student journals and logs, and reflections generated through personal and group evaluation.

AN ACTION RESEARCH APPROACH TO ENVIRONMENTAL PROBLEM SOLVING

WILLIAM B. STAPP
ARJEN E. J. WALS

Introduction

Halfway through the year at Lahser High School in Bloomfield Hills, Michigan, 10 juniors and seniors who have survived the first two rounds of projects are meeting for their experimental science class. Last week the students began the third set of projects by identifying areas of interest. Today they are giving each other feedback on their project ideas. Although instructors Dennis Travis and Greg Zogg played a significant role in the beginning, their input has become more subtle and individualized. Today, they are enjoying being observers.

"Now Katie," Mark says after a pause, "why would someone believe you, a high school junior, just because you say there is a garbage problem? Why would they just go out and start a program to recycle paper?" Katie is expecting the question and is ready with an answer.

"Because I will have data from similar projects. I will interview people in other school systems and offices that recycle material and purchase recycled things. If others have done it successfully, or can point out problems to avoid, how can they have excuses for sending ALL our garbage to the landfill?"

The class continues to review the other student projects, offering gentle advice and helpful ideas for each. Just before class ends, Greg asks the students to think about the session, guiding their thoughts to help them realize some of their new skills and abilities.

"We get more done in a day than before,"Krissy notes, "it's like we have more energy for the work we are doing."

"Don't you think that's because we have chosen these projects?" offers Katie. "I know I didn't care very much for that barnyard pond project we started with. Now that I'm working on something I really want to change, I like this class a lot."

Other students quickly agree, but they also admit they'd have been lost without the help the instructors provided on that first project. The barnyard pond project had walked them through the process of identifying a problem, collecting information, considering alternative solutions, making recommendations, and at each step, reflecting and revising their plan. The goal wasn't so much to help the farm manager with his polluted pond as it was to help the students learn a process of problem solving they could repeat with their own projects. Equally important, the experi-

ence forced them into groups and began to mold them from apathetic, independent teenagers to supportive partners. Today's interactions, for example, would have been more antagonistic and belligerent earlier in the term.

Katie's recycling project is a good example of how the process works. At the beginning of a project cycle, students think of the issues they really care about. In discussions with the class, they toss out suggestions for projects and form groups of students with similar interests. By the second week, the group presents a more coherent plan for the investigation of the problem and a solution. The members of the group develop that initial plan into a written project proposal that describes the nature of the problem, their expected or hypothesized outcome, and a timeline and methods needed for their investigation. The students revisit the plans frequently, sometimes changing them dramatically as more information becomes available.

Every Monday the students must provide an update to the entire class on their progress and outline their goals for the coming week. This is a time to solicit help and advice from their peers, learning from each other's successes and mistakes. During the week, each group meets with an instructor for a more intensive review of its project.

Katie realizes after her investigation that her ideal solution isn't practical. She changes her goal and the project results in a report and presentation to the school board, which decided to establish a pilot recycling program the next year. Because these projects started with student ideals, each project is forever colored with student expectations, energy, and values. After all, it's their education.

This chapter focuses on the process described here, Action Research and Community Problem Solving (AR&CPS). It is a well-rounded learning experience that allows teachers and students to work jointly towards the resolution of a problem of mutual concern. AR&CPS is an attempt to empower learners by involving them in planning and developing their own education and by letting them experience that action is possible, even on seemingly complicated tasks. It represents a systematic approach to learning that can equip learners with the experience and skills necessary to become confident and competent decision-makers in society.

We will discuss the two main components of AR&CPS: Action Research and Community Problem Solving, and provide a composite outline of an AR&CPS project in a formal education context. This composite outline is based on a variety of AR & CPS projects the University of Michigan's School of Natural Resources & Environment has facilitated at the elementary, middle, and high school level since 1985.

Action Research

Action Research in education has its beginnings in John Dewey's philosophy of reflective thinking (Dewey, 1963). Dewey criticized schools for separating thought from action and thinking from doing. He disliked the static curricula that characterized early twentieth century education with its rigid separation of the disciplines. Dewey emphasized that thought cannot be divorced from action. Therefore, school curricula should involve students in the real world with the aim of improving the community for everyone, "so that the future will be better than the past."

Action Research was first used, not in schools, but in social settings such as factories and housing projects. In the late 1930s and early 1940s, Kurt Lewin provided a concrete way to apply Dewey's philosophy by developing the methodology of Action Research. Lewin initially focused on the impacts of discrimination in the work place and the community (Lewin, 1946). Later, however, Lewin applied this approach to education when he worked with Stephen Corey of the Horace Mann-Lincoln Institute at Columbia University, to help teachers and teacher educators utilize Action Research in schools. In 1952 Corey spoke of the need for education to prepare citizens for a dramatically changing world. Education must change too, asserted Corey, but the changes should be developed within the schools by those individuals most directly affected.

> ...Our schools cannot keep up with the life they are supposed to sustain and improve unless teachers, pupils, supervisors, administrators, and school patrons continuously examine what they are doing. Singly and in groups, they must use their imaginations creatively and constructively to identify practices that must be changed to meet the needs and demands of modern life, courageously try out those practices that give better promise, and methodically and systematically give evidence to their worth. (Corey, 1953).

Action Research developed into a methodology that addresses problems in society by linking theories of change with practical action. It is designed to promote critical thinking at every stage of the process. To obtain a clearer understanding of Action Research we will now look at three major themes that emerge from Lewin's writings: Commitment to Democratic Principles, Praxis, and the Action Research Spiral (Lewin, 1946).

Commitment to Democratic Principles

Lewin, a social scientist, was interested in improving people's working and living conditions. He believed strongly in democratic decision making, a more equitable distribution of power, and practical problems as a never-failing source of ideas and knowledge (Lewin, 1946). Rather than asking for "outside" expertise to resolve existing disputes, Lewin involved the affected target group itself in articulating, discussing, and acting on a particular problem. Action Research is based on the assumption that people who are most affected by a social situation ought to be the ones evaluating it as well as the ones empowered to take action to change it. In factories, workers "on the line" would be the central characters. In schools, teachers, students, administrators, and parents take center stage.

The Action Research approach stands in stark contrast to the notion of "leaving it to the experts," a common response to problems in our high-tech world. While experts often have a valuable perspective on a problem, they may not know the problem firsthand or live with the consequences of actions they implement. Action Research posits that the people who live with a particular condition are usually more qualified to identify the problems associated with it and develop solutions that reflect their needs.

Praxis

In Action Research, evaluation, reflection, and action occur concurrently in a process that has become known as praxis, the union of reflection and action. While participants are engaged in a problem solving process, they are continuously reflecting on their work and evaluating its effectiveness. The process itself is an active one wherein participants, through analysis, conceptualization, fact finding, planning, execution, and evaluation—and then a repeat of this whole circle of activities—become engaged in a spiral process of task resolution, marked by critical reflection and action.

Notably, the Action Research approach has strong parallels to the ideas of Brazilian philosopher Paulo Freire, who has written extensively about the need for praxis and "conscientization." Conscientization is the process that moves an individual toward human liberation through critical consciousness of his or her state of oppression. This ultimately causes an individual to act in an effort to change his or her sociopolitical environment. Freire (1970) captured the spirit and philosophy of Action Research when he wrote:

> *You never really understand an issue or know how to help resolve it until you involve yourself in the issue. Then you begin to understand it, to identify the principal parties and actors involved, and begin to realize how to change it.*

The Action Research Spiral

Action Research is carried out in a series of repeated steps that can be diagrammed as a spiral (Figure 2:8). The process begins when participants (such as a teacher or a class of students) decide to address problems that affect them. By exploring, discussing, and negotiating with each other, Action Research participants identify and isolate a problem for study. They then work to understand the problem, to recognize the possibilities for resolving it, to explore the opportunities for taking action, and to identify the potential constraints that may impede their efforts.

As participants begin to generate ideas, they enter the first loop of the spiral. They develop a plan (**P**) that will help them solve their problem, implement that plan (**I**), and evaluate its effectiveness (**E**). Evaluation of the plan leads to the development of another plan, which takes them into the second loop, and the spiral continues. (The acronym for this spiral of repeated steps is **PIE.**) Loops generate more loops until the problem is resolved to the satisfaction of the participants. Throughout this process, participants reflect upon their learning and the evolution of the project. By reflecting, they can incorporate new information into their action strategy to better address their problem or to adjust their plan to a changing situation. Note that the action research spiral can be used at the individual level and at the group level, while the scope of the issue at stake can vary as well. The action research spiral also provides a useful metaphor to illustrate the nonlinear nature of problem solving and to emphasize the need for simultaneous action and reflection throughout the problem solving process.

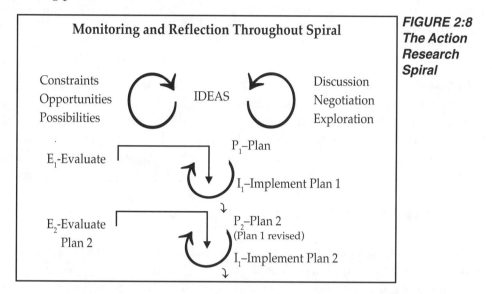

FIGURE 2:8 The Action Research Spiral

The utilization of Action Research in educational settings can take many forms (Carr, 1989). The focus of our work involves a melding of Action Research with Community Problem Solving in the context of environmental education.

Community Problem Solving

The Community Problem Solving component of AR&CPS has its origin in grassroots community organizing, efforts to help groups concerned about local problems and conditions to effect change. In the United States many community organizers have been trained at such places as the Highlander Center, and have in turn trained others. Today community organizing is a field in its own right.

In *Problem Solving: Concepts and methods for community organizations*, Brody (1982) covers the essentials for community organizers who work through the system. Major aspects of community problem solving and organizing that are critical to AR&CPS are explained below. In providing this information we draw on Brody's work.

The following are important elements of community problem solving: recognizing a problem; setting problem objectives; working in groups; collecting, organizing, and analyzing information; defining the problem from a variety of perspectives; identifying, considering, and selecting alternative actions to take; developing and carrying out a plan of action; coalition building; and evaluating the outcome and the entire process (Brody, 1982; Wals, Beringer, & Stapp, 1990). We will highlight some of these elements.

Defining the Problem

Brody points out that "a problem becomes a community problem when an individual's discontent becomes a broadly felt concern." Once that concern is expressed, it is important to define the problem. This is a critical step, for an ill-defined problem makes it difficult to focus on workable solutions and strategies to implement them. It is important not to define a problem in terms that suggest a solution, otherwise other solutions may not be considered. Once there is a narrow definition of the problem, it is very difficult to break out of that box to find other solutions.

To define a problem well there must first be an understanding of the background of the situation, which may require considerable probing. With this basic understanding it is then possible to write a problem statement with precision. General statements like, "Waste generation in the public schools is a problem" are valid expressions of concern, but are not helpful problem definitions, because the terms are ambiguous and solutions are difficult to generate. Problems should be stated clearly, such as "The use of Styrofoam in school cafeterias and the absence of in-school recycling contribute to the landfill problem in our community."

It is important to expand the definition to include answers to the basic questions: What is the problem? Where does it exist? Who is affected by it? When does it occur? To what degree is it felt? The next step then is to identify key factors affecting the problem, to focus on the problem area, and to assess the importance of the problem or part of the problem, and to analyze the potential for achieving an acceptable solution within a given time frame (what is working in our favor, or against us?). This way the community group is able to take into account the various dimensions of a problem.

Setting Problem Objectives

Once the problem has been well defined and priorities have been established, the next stage is to decide upon specific objectives. Objectives state exactly what your group wants to accomplish in a given period of time. If the problem is that a school does not accommodate recycling in the school building, then objectives could be to convince administrators, teachers and fellow students of the need for in-school recycling and to set up a system for collecting school waste that will facilitate the recycling of paper, cardboard, glass, aluminum, and toxins. It is important when setting problem objectives, that participants define potential successful outcomes of their project. Assessment of change is as important in setting community problem solving objectives as it is in setting business or educational objectives.

Working in Groups

This is a skill area that still appears to be underdeveloped in our society. Schools provide little training in working in groups and joint decision making so it is no surprise that community groups struggle with this. Individuals in the groups must learn to brainstorm effectively, to identify resources, to make decisions by consensus or voting, to recognize helpful and unhelpful group roles and behaviors, how to divide tasks among sub-groups, and how to implement change. These skills are so critical that participants may need to be trained to work together before they can begin addressing a community problem collaboratively.

Avoiding Pitfalls

Circular thinking makes it impossible to solve a problem and should be watched for and avoided. A good problem definition can help here. It is also important not to oversimplify a problem so as to avoid solutions that do not adequately address the problem. Another pitfall that groups sometimes fall into, which affects their credibility, is using analogies to prove that a problem exists, when only actual data are convincing. Another serious pitfall can be that the solution proposed is either too big or too small, and thus inappropriate to solving the problem. Not everything about problem solving can or should be rational. Sometimes we have to break out of the box to find a solution that works. Finally, the surest way for a group to fail in solving a community problem is to accept a palliative—an action that is not a real solution and addresses only the surface problem and not underlying causes. This is often referred to as the "band-aid approach." For instance, this is the case when a group is trying to solve the problem of street litter by organizing a street cleanup.

Coalition Building

Often one group by itself doesn't carry enough clout to give a problem the attention it deserves, let alone to solve it. Local environmentalists were upset about a proposed development in a park area in New York City. The group was unable to get the attention of city hall. But when it teamed up with a civil rights group and cast the issue as rich white folks trying to deny African Americans access to park areas, the city took notice and the combined groups were able to help solve the problem. Successful problem solving often involves finding where your group's interests intersect those of other groups and individuals who have political power or who by teaming together can draw more attention by sheer numbers.

Problem Analysis

To plan effective solutions and the strategies to get them implemented, there must be a good underlying problem analysis. Answers to the following questions must be found: Who are the actors in this problem arena? Who is affected and in what way? Who is responsible for creating the problem? Who has power to correct it? Who might be against your solution and how might you answer their arguments? What is your power in this situation and how can it be used? Problem analysis helps groups plan effective problem solving strategies.

Designing an Action Plan

A good action plan names, defines, and documents the problem. It presents an analysis of causes, the situation as it is now, and the costs of continuing this way. It suggests alternative solutions and the costs of each along with the benefits, and a recommendation of one solution with a rationale. The action plan also breaks up the effort to solve the problem into concrete tasks, each with its own time line and person or persons responsible for accomplishing that task. Goals and objectives are set and priorities are also decided upon.

Having presented some of the theoretical foundations that helped shape our approach to environmental problem solving in schools, we will now turn to the model itself. We should note that the word "model" may be inappropriate here, since it suggests that it is a set of rules and guidelines that can be copied universally. This notion undermines our philosophy which holds that members of the school community should be allowed to play an essential role in developing, implementing, evaluating, and re-developing their own so-called models.

The Synthesis:
Action Research & Community Problem Solving

Students are sometimes dissatisfied with their education and unmotivated in the classroom because they feel that what they learn is removed from, and not useful or valid in, the "real world" (Everhart, 1983). The AR&CPS approach attempts to avert this discrepancy by addressing problems that students are confronted with on a daily basis. It is no surprise that during the AR&CPS process, institutional barriers to this kind of education often become a focus of attention. Teachers, students, administrators, and parents inevitably will be challenged by the institutional constraints that need to be changed for schools to be more responsive to education that is of an interdisciplinary nature, involves the use of community resources, transforms the teacher-student relationship, and leads to action taking.

Through AR&CPS, students' own experience and perception of the world become the focal point of their education. By synthesizing action research and community problem solving we have arrived at a learning process that enables students and teachers to participate more fully in the planning, implementing, and evaluating of educational activities aimed at resolving an environmental issue that the learners have identified. Note that the meaning of the construct "environmental issue" depends on the perceptions and the experiences of the learner as well as on the context in which education takes place. The term "environment" thus is broadly defined to include political, social, economic, and bio/physical aspects.

During the AR&CPS process, students are given responsibility in planning educational activities and are provided with the opportunity to take responsible action toward improving the quality of their community environment. Students become the practitioners of their own education when they take on the role of explorers, researchers, theorists, planners, and actors. They come to assume more responsibility for their own learning. The teacher becomes the guide and facilitator in this process and shares the role of learner when reflecting upon his or her own teaching practices and when learning about the issue in which the students immerse themselves.

Several presuppositions underlie this approach to education. First, it is crucial for society to solve critical issues with the full participation of its young members. Second, students need to know that they can be forces for constructive change and that their involvement is indeed needed in the world. Third, giving students a chance to investigate and act on a problem of their own choice will increase their motivation to learn. Last, the school and its community contain an abundance of rich material—of printed matter (newspapers, books, magazines), human resources (students, teachers, parents, institutions, organizations), equipment (chemical analysis kits, water monitoring devices, computers), for making education more meaningful to the students.

Basic Steps in Action Research and Community Problem Solving

In this section some basic steps or stages that can be distinguished in AR&CPS are described. These steps are presented here in a linear and logical order for clarity. It should be noted that the steps as outlined in this section do not necessarily occur as depicted. How teacher and students undertake these steps and in what sequence will vary with the individual and collective needs of all people involved in a project.

Planning the Process
Given the structure of schooling, it is quite a challenge to find a group of teachers and administrators who are willing to critically investigate their own educational practices and to develop their own curriculum. One of several ways to introduce the AR&CPS approach to a school is to organize a one-day workshop for teachers, administrators, and, when possible, students and parents. Ideally, in the spirit of action research, such a workshop would be initiated and facilitated by teachers and administrators within the school community, but schools may want to utilize support from outside resources as well (e.g., local teacher colleges, schools of education, and community groups).

The initial workshop should focus on questions like: What are some of the short-comings in our educational program? How can we address them? How can we involve the students? and not on the question, What is AR&CPS? During discussion, some of the underlying principles and guiding assumptions of AR&CPS are likely to surface and can be adapted to the special needs and requirements of the school and its community. These consultation sessions will nurture a cooperative approach to the AR&CPS project and will help the teachers gain the support of the school's critical community (i.e., the principal, librarian, colleagues, parents).

Teachers working with AR&CPS need support from their colleagues as this approach to education involves the handing over of some of the control—sometimes obtained after a long struggle—of the classroom process to the students, working with an open-ended curriculum geared toward action taking, and evaluating the learners using journal entries and participation levels as guidelines. During the workshop the participants can discuss what kind of support they will need from administration, colleagues, and parents.

By the end of the workshop, a decision should be made whether and how to conduct an AR&CPS project. Teachers and administrators should select a class or classes in which to implement the project. If the class schedule lends itself to linking content areas (e.g., natural and social sciences), a team teaching approach across subjects and disciplines can be selected. Participants should also decide on a kind of support mechanism. One support mechanism could be to set up a regular meeting time where participating teachers can share their experiences with administration and colleague teachers. Such a meeting would give others within the school a better sense of what an AR&CPS project is all about, while it would provide the participating faculty with important support and feedback.

After the teacher(s) and school administrators agree to conduct an AR&CPS project, the students in the selected class are introduced to the project and asked whether they would be interested in participating. If so, parents are informed via the students and a letter from the teacher(s). The initial planning phase culminates with the teacher(s) establishing a tentative time line for the AR&CPS project. Teachers, administrators, and other interested parties may decide to set up an AR&CPS committee to guide the project.

Assessing Student Skills

At the onset and throughout the project, the teacher assesses the students' problem solving skills. If certain competencies are lacking, exercises can be done prior to and during the project to learn and refine these skills. A teacher could look at *group process skills* (e.g., the ability to listen with comprehension, to reduce "isms" such as racism and sexism, to provide constructive feedback, and to work toward group consensus), at information gathering skills (e.g., the ability to carry out a survey, to use a newspaper, to write a letter, to interview people, to find and contact agencies and organizations), and at more general problem-solving skills (e.g., the ability to work effectively as a member of a group; to recognize, identify, and state a problem; to generate, evaluate, and select alternative solutions; and to develop, implement, and evaluate a plan of action). Each of these skills can be enhanced through specific classroom activities (Bull et al., 1988).

Selecting a Topic

An AR&CPS project can begin with a walking and/or bus tour of the school and its neighborhood. The goal of this tour is to increase students' awareness of the natural and social environment of their community, which aids in exploring potential project topics. Students record issues of concern in individual notebooks. The neighborhood walk can be supplemented with a tour of the school building and grounds, where issues of student concern are also noted.

During the AR&CPS class sessions following the walk and/or bus tour(s), recorded topics are compiled through brainstorming environmental problems that students have become familiar with in their school, neighborhood, and community. The generation of topics can be done by small groups or by the class as a whole. The issues should be recorded in a class log book, which is to become a constant companion throughout the AR&CPS project.

The list of problems that appear on the board is often long and may address immediate as well as long-term concerns, local as well as global environmental issues. We already pointed out that in AR&CPS, the term "environment" is very broadly understood to encompass both the natural and social environment. For instance, in one of the AR&CPS projects conducted in Detroit, Michigan, students listed concerns which included abandoned houses that are used to sell crack, street gangs and related violence, lack of trees and flowers, litter on the streets, poor quality public housing, students being killed in car accidents on their way to school, and teenage pregnancy.

Once critical problems have been identified, the groups or class might cluster the topics and generate a set of criteria with which to narrow down their list. Urgency, critical nature of the problem, access to information, not too complex, and of interest to us have been criteria used by students in the past. These criteria help them discuss the various topics and decide which problem(s) to research. The outcome of this selection process may be one AR&CPS project for the entire class or several topics to be addressed in small groups (e.g., one to three projects with 6 to 7 students per group). This, too, is left to the students and teachers to decide collaboratively.

An AR&CPS project uses a class log book and individual student journals for written documentation of the learning process. The class log gives a detailed, technical daily account of the project and provides guidelines for further tasks, responsibilities, and research while the individual journals give students an outlet for their emotional response to their education, linking cognitive and affective learning and developing writing skills. Questions they might address include "How does being involved in this project affect me?" "How does this project affect my classmates and the teacher?" "What things do I like about the project?" "What things do I dislike about it?" and "How can we improve the project?" It is important that teachers also keep a journal addressing similar questions, but also questions related to changes they see occurring in their teaching and the school as an institution.

Researching the Topic

After the final topic(s) have been selected, the students research the topic in order to develop a problem statement that defines their project clearly. Parallel to the phases of community problem solving mentioned in the previous section—but not necessarily in the same order—students become engaged in defining the problem, setting problem objectives (project outcomes), group decision making, avoiding pitfalls, coalition building, problem analysis, designing a plan of action, and identifying and evaluating alternatives. In past AR&CPS projects, we have found that students, once a project topic has been selected, have a tendency to jump to quick ad hoc solutions. To avoid disappointment and find workable solutions, it is important that the students research the topic to gain a deeper understanding of the problem.

Throughout the project, the teacher serves as a facilitator; a source of information, a coordinator of group activities and field trips who provides, in conjunction with the administration and other teachers, materials the students want to use. In this research phase, students may work with newspaper articles; the school and public library; the yellow pages of the local telephone directory; a school computer; and human resources such as parents, administrators, other teachers, and local agencies. The information obtained is documented in the class log book and shared with all group members.

Determining Action

Once the students feel they have collected enough information about the problem under study, the AR&CPS project enters the action phase. While research continues, the project's action component, again, requires brainstorming a list of alternative strategies for addressing the problem, and establishing criteria with which to narrow down alternatives to one plan that students will implement to effect the change they desire.

A very important element of action phase is defining the outcome or "success" of the project. The nature of the problem outlines the potential scope of action and resolution. For instance, "it would be too pretentious to think that a group of students from inner city Detroit could solve the problem of drug abuse" (Wals & Stapp, 1989, p. 237). Therefore, it is crucial to discuss with students what is reasonably possible in the long and short run. In most situations the point is not that students completely resolve a problem (although this has been done), but that they take effective action to alleviate it.

Considering the action-reflection spiral (Figure 2:8), the action plan can be modified and refined until it meets the students' criteria of success. Again the individual journal becomes instrumental in providing students with an opportunity to articulate feelings of success and failure (Wals, 1989). Eventually, the consequences of the project are reported to all involved and interested parties: parents, teachers, the school, the community, and maybe the local press. The teachers themselves go through a similar process during which they articulate their own experiences with the project. Their written account of the project could include a description of how the project affected their teaching; their relationship with students, parents, and administrative personnel; and suggestions for further improvement of future AR&CPS projects including those pertaining to institutional change (creating team-teaching opportunities, modifying class schedules, considering alternative student assessment techniques, obtaining access to community resources, changing school policies, etc.).

Evaluation

Evaluation of the project is an ongoing element in all phases of AR&CPS. The log book, used to record achievements of past AR&CPS sessions and to write the agenda for coming project periods, gives a detailed account of the accomplished work. Individual journals serve as a medium for students to express their feelings and reactions to the AR&CPS process, which can help the teacher in modifying the project.

In addition, teachers periodically use other evaluative techniques such as "Plus, Minus, Change Sheets," which is a tool to get students to reflect on the things they like, dislike, and would change about the project. The teachers' documented observations can become the basis for a discussion on the strengths and shortcomings of the project with members of the AR&CPS support committee. These discussions with colleagues might result in additional constructive feedback (Bryant, 1988).

With regard to individual students' evaluation, the philosophy behind AR&CPS is founded on the belief that students will develop skills and become empowered as a result of their experience with the project. Empowerment here means that students, having been given responsibility for the planning of their own education and the opportunity to investigate and act upon an issue that concerns them, obtain the feeling that they can have an impact on decisions that affect their lives. Although one can have a false sense of empowerment, it seems that talent and knowledge go much further in solving problems if one has self-confidence. Students' verbal statements and written journal entries are instrumental in detecting feelings of empowerment or disempowerment and can help the teacher in readjusting the project and/or spending more time with a particular student.

As a day-to-day process, the growth and learning that occurs in AR&CPS cannot be measured with a grade on the culminating action alone. A student's contribution in all stages of the project should be considered in the evaluation. Teachers in past projects have used several criteria on which to base a grade including effort put into journal writing, quality of student reports, level of class participation, ability to work in a small group, quality of oral reports, and student self-evaluation. Although assigning a grade seems inevitable, most action-research-based approaches in education maintain that the purpose of evaluation is not to assess, judge, and compare students, but to give them feedback that stimulates further learning.

Conclusion

We have presented an alternative approach to education in the form of Action Research & Community Problem Solving. Action Research is the process wherein participants, through analysis, conceptualization, fact finding, planning, execution, and evaluation—and then a repetition of this whole cycle of activities—become engaged in a spiral process of task resolution, marked by critical reflection and action. Community Problem Solving can be defined as the process that helps groups concerned about local problems and conditions to become more effective in effecting change. Applied to the formal education system, the synthesis between the two results in a process that enables students and teachers to participate more fully in planning, implementing, and evaluating educational activities aimed at resolving an issue that the learners have identified. AR&CPS allows students' own ideas to be at the center of the curriculum. By acting on their own ideas, AR&CPS gives students the opportunity to realize that they can be forces of constructive change. Hereby, students learn that they can act responsibly and effectively rather than being acted upon. In its totality, AR&CPS affirms students' value in shaping a quality future.

References

Brody, R. (1982). *Problem solving: Concepts and methods for community organizations.* New York: Human Sciences Press.

Bryant, B. (1988). *Quality circles: New management strategies for schools.* Ann Arbor, MI: Prakken Publications, Inc..

Bull, J., Cromwell, M., Cwikiel, W., DiChiro, G., Guarino, J., Rathje, R., Stapp, W., Wals, A.E., & Youngquist, M. (1988). *Education in action: A community problem solving program for schools.* Dexter, MI: Thomson-Shore.

Carr, W. (1989). Action research: Ten years on. *Journal of Curriculum Studies* 21(1): 85-90.

Carr, W., & Kremmis, S. (1986). *Becoming critical: Education, knowledge and action research.* London: Falmer Press.

Corey, S.M. (1953). *Action research to improve school practices.* New York: Teachers College.

Dewey, J. (1963). *Experience and education.* New York: Collier Books.

DiChiro, G. & Stapp, W.B. (1986). *Education in action: An action research approach to environmental problem solving.* In Perkins, J.H., Alexis, D., and Bauer, K. (Eds.), *Monographs in environmental education and environmental studies (Vol. III).* Troy, OH: The North American Association for Environmental Education (NAAEE).

Eisner, E.W. (1991). *The enlightened eye: Qualitative inquiry and the enhancement of educational practice.* New York: Macmillan.

Everhart, R.B. (1983). *Reading, writing and resistance.* Boston: Routledge & Kegan Paul.

Freire, P. (1970). *Pedagogy of the oppressed.* New York: Continuum.

Hustler, D., Cassidy, A., & Cuff, E.C. (1986). *Action research in classrooms and schools.* London: Allen & Unwin.

Lewin, K. (1946). Action research and minority problems. *Journal of Social Issues* 26: 3-23.

McTaggart, R., et al. (1982). *The action research planner.* Waurn Ponds, Victoria, Australia.

Wals, A. (1989). *Education in action: A community problem solving model for schools.* Report to the William T. Grant Foundation on the Use of Journals in Evaluating AR&CPS in Two Detroit Middle Schools. Ann Arbor: University of Michigan.

Wals, A. & Stapp, W.B. (1989). Education in action: A community problem solving program for schools. In Iozzi, L.A. and Shepard, C.L. (Eds.) *Building multicultural webs through environmental education: 1988 NAAEE conference proceedings.* Troy, OH: NAAEE

Wals, A.E.J., Beringer, A., & Stapp, W.B. (1990). Education in action: a community problem solving program for schools. *Journal for Environmental Education* 21(4): 13-20.

Winter, R. (1989). *Learning from experience: Principles and practice in action research.* New York: Falmer Press.

MODELS AND APPROACHES : PART 4

EDITORS' INTRODUCTION

Beyond the Model/Module Mentality in Environmental Problem Solving: Ian Robottom

Robottom advocates an environmental issue problem solving process in which students develop their own response to an issue. Robottom cites three international experiences supporting his concept of community-based education, where students work on controversial issues and are allowed to develop knowledge through an issue investigation that steers the curriculum. This type of experience results in an emerging curriculum that Robottom maintains eliminates the need for a directed curriculum. This responsive approach is based on the assumption that since environmental issues do not have predictable outcomes, the curriculum to prepare for such idiosyncratic situations cannot be prescribed. Robottom emphasizes the need to value the knowledge and skills students develop from unstructured investigations. The teacher facilitates the process by monitoring and organizing the emerging activities, and, therefore, is in an excellent position to undertake original research on the educational process. Students and teachers are expected to reflect on the process and allow for new understanding to change their perceptions of the problem. The role of teacher and his or her continual professional growth during this collaborative environmental inquiry are key to Robottom's approach. Table 2:5 summarizes Robottom's approach and is followed by his description of and support for an unstructured community problem solving process.

Note: A table of comparisons does not fit with the paradigm Robottom describes. However the author is willing to have his approach represented in the table having acknowledged the paradigm differences.

References

Greenall Gough, A. & Robottom, I. (1993). Towards a socially critical environmental education: Water quality studies in a coastal school. *Journal of Curriculum Studies* 25(2).

Muhlebach, R. & Robottom, I. (1990). *Environmental education and computer conferences project: Supporting community-based environmental education.* Geelong, Victoria: Deakin Institute for Studies on Education.

O'Donoghue, R. & McNaught, C. (1991). Environmental education: the development of a curriculum through 'grass-roots' reconstructive action. *International Journal of Science Education* 13(4): 391–404.

What Happens in the Classroom

Students and teachers jointly explore and work on a local controversial issue. Students undertake original research and generate new working knowledge about the issue. Students critically examine and appraise the relationship of community and environment and contribute their assessment as part of wider community debate about the issue. Teachers are intimately involved in assessing and changing their approaches and roles and participate in researching their contribution to the inquiry.

Assumptions about Problem Solving

This is a community-based critical environmental inquiry. The problem is idiosyncratic and one cannot predict how to address the problem before the process. Problem solving is a practical activity—we learn through a process of praxis, reflecting critically on the meaning of our own interventions. The process and the needed skills emerge as participants adopt a perspective on their own role as problem-solvers. Constant evaluation and reflection allow for these skills to be developed.

Learning

The process of investigation is an action in and of itself. Action is not the desired end; social change, or change in the relationship between community and environment, is. Considering the relationship of community to environment is an interdisciplinary process where several perspectives are used to analyze the situation.

Teaching Strategies

The teacher collaborates with students, reflecting with students on the process and situation. The teacher may use the opportunity to research his or her own practice and how to organize educational experiences enabling problem solving.

Students' Role and Involvement

Students undertake original research, learn by experience, and collaborate with teachers and community. There are numerous successful instances at both elementary and secondary schools. Whole class groups are involved at one time.

Evaluation Strategies

An ongoing process of constant reflective evaluation maintains a high quality of original research and skill development that emerges from unstructured investigation. The experiences are evaluated in response to emerging curriculum, not to preordained objectives.

TABLE 2:5
Summary of the Robottom Environmental Issue Problem-Solving Approach

BEYOND THE MODEL/MODULE MENTALITY
IN ENVIRONMENTAL PROBLEM SOLVING

IAN ROBOTTOM

The brief account below outlines an instance of the kind of problem solving environmental education I would want to support. This account is drawn from a recent article by Greenall Gough and Robottom (1993) and sets the scene for consideration of a general set of principles relating to problem solving in environmental education.

Queenscliff High School, a relatively large school in a coastal holiday resort town, began its environmental education activities with a study of freshwater quality. In response to local imperatives, it changed the focus of its research to a critical study of sewage pollution of the nearby swimming and surfing beaches.

This school's involvement in water quality studies was in part a response to concerns expressed within the student body and within the community at large about the obvious sewage pollution of nearby beaches. These beaches are widely known for their swimming, surfing, and fishing opportunities, and there was an increasing community concern about the amounts of disposable items (such as plastic syringes and condoms) and sewage finding their way onto the beaches. The school developed a research program (nominally within Year 11 Marine Studies and Year 12 Biology) beginning with studies of the sand dunes along the foreshore and including tests of bacteria levels in the ocean. The school's investigations showed that coliform bacteria counts far in excess of acceptable Environmental Protection Authority (Victoria) guidelines for safe body contact were common in the seawater where thousands of people swim, surf, and fish on a regular basis.

Prior to going public with the results of their investigations by providing their data to the mass media, the students and teachers attempted to discuss the issue with the local Water Board but were rebuffed. The water board controls a large, new sewage treatment plant that voids its effluent into the ocean via an outfall located offshore from the popular swimming, surfing, and fishing beaches. The water board had previously been invited to participate in the school's study in an advisory capacity (for example, by contributing technical expertise via the computer conference), but had also declined. Following these rebuffs the school invoked the state government's Freedom of Information Act to gain access to the water board's own records of bacteria levels.

Early in 1989 the school published an account of its activities and their outcomes in the local press (The Geelong Advertiser *3 February 1989: 1):*

Testing of bacteria levels from Thirteenth Beach to Ocean Grove has revealed readings up to 40 times above a safe limit. The tests, taken by Queenscliff High School students during December, were done before the Geelong and District Water Board started commissioning its $32 million sewage outfall. The teacher said he had been refused access to the water board's figures and had lodged a Freedom of Information request so he could compare the readings.

This disclosure triggered a powerful response from several sections of the community: Local, state and national print and electronic media ran stories publicizing the school's activities, the issue itself, and its relationship to other instances of marine pollution elsewhere in the country. The local surfriders' association aligned itself with the school in criticizing the state of local beaches, specifically in terms of sewage pollution (The Age 27 February 1989: 15):

> *The state government would insist on further work being done on a new sewage treatment plant, forcing Geelong sewage into Bass Strait, if the plant failed to meet Environmental Protection Authority objectives, the minister for Planning and Environment, Mr. Roper, said today....."The president of the Thirteenth Beach Surf Lifesaving Club, Mr. Brett Cooper, said last night that, despite the new treatment plant, club members continued to find syringes, condoms, and plastic along the beach. 'We've found enough for truckloads,' he said. 'And we are concerned about the pollution also because some readings obtained by Queenscliff High School as part of an education department program at the outfall show the E.coli count is 40 times higher than permissible levels.'"*

The local health center began to maintain records of complaints about infections and illnesses possibly associated with the bacteria present in the seawater. Funding support for the school's project activities was forthcoming from Victoria's Ministry of Education, a regional education/industry collaborative, and the State Rural Water Commission. Some of the other schools participating in the project shifted the emphasis of their investigations from freshwater quality to seawater bacteria levels at beaches close to their communities.

In short, the school's activities were at least partly responsible for mobilizing a general and sustained community interest in this issue. One outcome of this increased public consciousness was a requirement for the water board to justify its environmental actions in regard to this issue. Ultimately, the Victorian Minister for Environment and Planning asked the water board to undertake substantial improvements to their sewage treatment facility, at a likely cost of more than $5 million (The Geelong News 27 June 1989: 3):

> *The state government last night told the Geelong and District Water Board its new $30 million Black Rock sewage outfall is not good enough. Planning and Environment Minister, Mr. Tom Roper, in Drysdale last night, said the Government would step into the ongoing*

dispute over the outfall. While the outfall has undoubtedly improved the situation, significant concerns remain. It is clear additional works are required. Board corporate services manager, Mr. Rob Jordan, said the board was "bound to disagree" with some of Mr. Roper's comments. Responding, Mr. Roper said, "Disagree as much as you like. You will be cleaning up your water."

Introduction

A common pattern in environmental education is to base environmental problem solving on a set of curriculum development/skill development materials imported from outside the actual environmental education context made up of school and environs. My intention in this contribution is to outline three instances of environmental problem solving, and from these to derive a set of general principles about environmental problem solving. I will also be considering deeper issues concerning the relationship of research with environmental problem solving and the way in which the traditional preoccupation with "models" and "modules" tends to prefigure our thinking in environmental problem solving.

The Environment and School Initiatives Project Coordinated by the Organization for Economic Cooperation and Development (OECD), Paris

The OECD's Center for Educational Research and Innovation (CERI) currently coordinates a research project in environmental education involving 20 member countries of the OECD, the majority of which are European.

At its simplest, the research portrays instances of increasingly significant community-based, environment-related curriculum development and investigates the ways in which the professional development demands associated with such work are met. Australia is a participant in this OECD project. Our project is yielding case studies of community-based environmental curriculum and professional development at the time that state policies in environmental education are emerging and national policies are being considered (AJEE, 1991).

The specific aims of the Australian project are to:

1. Explore the relationship between recent state and national education policies and current and emerging school initiatives in community-based environmental education;

2. Explore the relationship between current approaches to professional development and emerging school initiatives in community-based environmental education;

3. Develop a series of case studies that present contextualised descriptions of the relationships among policy, curriculum development practices, and professional development.

In Australia, methods used to develop these case studies include personal interviews, professional diaries, document analysis, and analysis of the archive of published teacher-prepared material. Teachers and students in certain Victorian schools have been writing accounts of their own experiences in this project (Armstrong, 1990; Bird, 1990; Shepherd & Norman, 1990; Wills, 1990; Wood, 1990). The case studies describe a range of community-based curriculum development activities undertaken by Victorian schools; a number of pedagogical and curriculum issues that arose in association with these activities; and the various forms of support teachers and students found useful in maintaining and developing their community-based curriculum work. These included new roles adopted by, and required of, educational support agencies.

Project research focuses on the generation of local knowledge as part of community-based environmental education curriculum development and addresses questions such as:

- How does the role of teachers change?

- What alternatives to the traditional view of curriculum content or knowledge are evident?

- What counts as proper knowledge?

- What new forms of communication between support persons, teachers, students, and parents develop?

- What alternatives are evident regarding the traditional roles of educational and non-educational agencies?

- What benefits for the teaching of traditional disciplines have emerged?

- In what terms do teachers justify or legitimate their involvement?

- What alternative forms of assessment are used and how are they justified?

This research project is reported in more detail in Posch (1988), Elliott (1991), and Robottom (1991).

The Environmental Education and Computer Conference Project in Australia
This collaborative environmental education project involving six schools, Deakin University, school support centers, and several government and local community agencies is now winding down. It gained its initial inspiration from similar work at the University of Michigan under the leadership of Professor William Stapp. The project played a significant role in raising community awareness about a serious environmental issue, that of sewerage pollution of popular nearby beaches. Through its work, the project has also engaged a number of other significant educational issues.

The project had three overlapping dimensions. First, students and teachers in the six participating schools were involved in environmental enquiries into local controversial environmental issues. Second, students and teachers were involved in exploring the use of a computer conference in their environmental science enquiries. The schools' microcomputers were coupled through modems to the Deakin mainframe computer and thence to a computer conference housed at The University of Michigan. This link enabled interaction between students in several countries. Third, participants in the project adopted a research perspective, reflecting on a range of technical, teaching, and curriculum issues that arose through work in the other two dimensions (Robottom & Hart, 1990).

The role computers played in this project varied in the participating schools, but tended to support the main activity of environmental inquiry. The computers were seen as tools with the potential of improving the scientific aspects of environmental inquiry by expanding the "community of scientific inquirers" (Robottom & Muhlebach, 1989).

An assumption was that a curriculum based on critical environmental inquiry and the use of an international computer conference represented a significant challenge to existing teaching and curriculum practice in schools. It was felt the best way of dealing with this challenge was to look at both the emerging educational and the environmental issues from a research perspective. Teachers and other participants were encouraged to maintain professional diaries and other records of their project life.

Another aspect was for teachers to exploit the potential in the project to gain support from other participants and government and community agencies. Thus the project adopted a responsive, open agenda, allowing an interactive link between professional development (participatory educational research) and school-based curriculum development (the environmental enquiries). Technical, teaching, and curriculum issues were addressed as they emerged and were described in teachers' written reports, some of which were published.

The following were some of the issues addressed in this project:

- The role an international computer conference can play in expanding the scientific community allowing young people in small isolated rural schools to collaborate with a larger number of co-investigators in other schools engaging in similar enquiries.

- The variety of ways in which students use the computer conference.

- The effect the availability of the computer conference as an alternative source of solutions has on teacher-student relationships in the classroom.

- The significant role teachers and students each play in raising community awareness of environmental issues.

- The possibility of a curriculum based on emergent working knowledge rather than on predetermined textual knowledge.

- The variety of interactive forms of communications required in collaborative participatory research.

This research is reported in more detail in Robottom & Muhlebach (1989), Muhlebach & Robottom (1990), Robottom & Hart (1990) and Greenall Gough & Robottom (1993).

Grassroots Reconstructive Action in South Africa: The Action Ecology Project
O'Donoghue & McNaught (1991) describe a curriculum development study, the "Action Ecology" project, which "set out to improve science fieldwork by developing materials for an environmental education approach to ecology fieldwork" (p. 394). The study began as a research and development initiative to improve environmental education. It was initially informed by an instrumental, center-periphery, research-development-dissemination-adoption (RDDA) model of curriculum change. However, despite apparently successful workshops as a dissemination strategy, it was found that the curriculum packages were not widely used.

The following are some of the emerging environmental education issues encountered:

- pupils treated ecology as a body of scientific facts to be discovered in nature reserves;

- fieldwork data collection frequently involved mindless measurement, and hands-on and minds-on teacher-contrived worksheets;

- excursions were often dominated by show-and-tell activities by teachers and conservation experts.

Over a period of two years the project organizers transformed the project in fundamental ways, including the methodologies it subscribed to, the research and evaluation styles it applied, the style of workshops, and the design and status of curriculum support materials. The rationalist, center-periphery orientation of the original research and development project was replaced by a teacher support network to encourage grassroots reconstructive action.

Project organizers noted three important trends in this transformation:

1. Outlook (pedagogy and didactics): a swing from the determinism of a positivist and behaviorist perspective to an interpretive position centered on social theory and experiential learning.

2. Approach (research and workshops): a swing from external problem solving and resource development to a support service for teacher-centered reflection and change.

3. Design (materials and management): a move from external management of pretested, objective-centered packages developed by a project team, to a resource pool and networking support service for teachers to adapt and develop resources to local needs (O'Donoghue & McNaught, 1991, p. 398).

These trends are similar to the features reported from the Greenall Gough & Robottom (1993) project, "Environmental Education and Computer Conference."

Learning From Experience:
Some Principles of Environmental Problem Solving

The experience gained in projects such as these tends to support a number of propositions about environmental education in general and environmental problem solving in particular.

Environmental problem solving should entail investigation of local environmental issues. Environmental problem solving works best in cases where students explore environmental issues accessible to them in terms of geography and scale. The best local environmental issues are those which the students identify as being of interest and concern to them.

Environmental problem solving should be inquiry based.
Environmental problem solving should entail by students some original research into a local environmental issue. There should be opportunities for enquiries to generate new working knowledge (Greenall Gough & Robottom, 1993) about the issue in question. This has implications for what is to be valued as proper curriculum content, because the predetermined, systematic, disciplinary knowledge found in texts is less "authoritative" and compelling than the new knowledge generated by participants in their investigation of the issue (Greenall Gough & Robottom, 1993).

Environmental problem solving should be critical.
The enquiries conducted by students should include appraisal of the environmental, social, and other values within the contending proposals for action. Any environmental issue, by definition, is constituted of differing points of view. And every proposal for action can only be understood in terms of certain assumptions about the way communities and environments ought to relate to each other. Environmental education that aims to improve students' understanding of how environmental problems are resolved is inadequate unless it creates the conditions for students to appraise and critique those assumptions.

Environmental problem solving should be community based.
As argued earlier (Robottom, 1987) environmental education is doubly idiosyncratic: "the environmental issues that form part of the substance of environmental education work are usually specific in terms of time and space .... and educational problems are rarely susceptible to universal solutions" (p. 297). In the case of

environmental problem solving outlined earlier, the nature of the curriculum work was determined by the nature of the unfolding environmental issues, which only have meaning within the community in which the issues are constructed. For example, the issue of fecal coliform levels in seawater had meaning as a health risk to students engaging in after-school and weekend surfing at a nearby beach. Its resolution reached by sustained investigation and publication of water quality could only have turned out as it did within the framework of existing community agencies and media services in the township (Greenall Gough & Robottom, 1993).

Environmental problem solving should be collaborative.

The projects, especially the second, illustrate the political character of environmental problem solving. Students engaging in the investigation of fecal contamination of surfing beaches encountered resistance from the local water board, but political support from the media, local surfriders' association, and other schools. In the end, the state minister for the environment demanded a review of water board operations. This action resulted in a $50 million restructuring of wastewater disposal in the area, which confirms the political character of this kind of curriculum work. This experience demonstrates the need for and effectiveness of collaborative action, rather than individual efforts.

The outcome of environmental problem solving is unpredictable.

Environmental problem solving in schools is unpredictable and unforeseeable at two levels. The substantive (environmental) issues are a function of the environmental, social, political, and historical context within which an aspect of the environment is seen as problematic; and the methodological (inquiry) issues are shaped and change over time in response to emerging and evolving understandings about the relationship between "issue" and "solution." As participants explore a particular issue, their understandings of that issue change. Similarly, as their understandings of the issue change, the adequacy of their initial investigations to solve the issue also change and need to be improved. This fact is startlingly demonstrated in the South African Action Ecology instance already described. An important corollary of this unpredictability and the responsiveness it necessitates is that it is nonsense to try to separate a single generalizable process of problem solving into a single model that can be applied irrespective of the nature of the environmental issue in question.

Environmental problem solving should avoid the centralized, deterministic strategies of the model approach.

The deterministic center-to-periphery ideology of educational management needs to be replaced with an approach that eschews deterministic 'models' in favor of creating conditions for a responsive, collaborative, community-based critique. O'Donoghue & McNaught (1991, p. 402) offer some features of such an approach:

1. A research team working with groups of teachers as co-researchers.

2. Description, criticism, and exchange of fieldwork techniques and resource materials.

3. Interpretation and discussion of environmental education and environmental issues.

4. Creation of environmental education activities or selection and adoption of materials from a resource pool.

5. External moderation mechanisms to overcome possible contextual constraints.

Beyond The Determinism of Models and Modules

The tradition for environmental problem solving is to adopt a model mentality, an approach to curriculum development that imposes external, allegedly scientific, rational and objective research processes of the research-development-dissemination-adoption (RDDA) model of curriculum change. Centrally designed skill development modules aimed at teaching teachers and students how to engage in environmental problem solving tend to be touted as the answer to successful environmental problem solving. The three instances outlined above demonstrate that abilities in environmental problem solving are more idiosyncratic than assumed in the model/module approach. They are shaped by the exigencies of the particular investigation, and are 'learned' through the investigation process rather than being taught by some predetermined skill development modules developed on a RDDA model. As O'Donoghue & McNaught (1991, p. 393) point out, 'develop and implement' approaches to change have, unfortunately, proved to be surprisingly weak (Papagiannis, Kless, & Bickel 1982; Popkewitz, 1984). The irony is that because such modules claim a strong empirical research base (they claim virtually to be proven effective), their failure has most often been ascribed to teacher- and school-related factors such as communication weaknesses and lack of teacher commitment rather than to inadequacies of the modules themselves. Yet it is possible that the "key failings of prevailing approaches to curriculum development can be traced to flaws in the underlying assumptions of deterministic models of change, (to) the assumption that the management of change through external and rational processes of curriculum development is both possible and desirable" (O'Donoghue & McNaught, 1991, p. 393).

One assumption concerns the relationship between research and environmental problem solving implicit in RDDA models. In such models, research is regarded as what the academy does to get its modules right so that teachers and students can be taught environmental problem solving. In the three experiences reported earlier, any research the academy might have done to establish the bona fides of a particular set of skill development modules is insignificant in comparison with the research that teachers and students do in their environmental problem solving. The important research is carried out by teachers and students to reach a resolution of the environmental problem at hand and a resolution of how to organize educational experiences to enable environmental problem solving to take place.

Another assumption concerns what are valued knowledge and skills. One option (assumed in the model/module approach) is for members of the academy to identify a predetermined, systematic body of knowledge and skills accepted as useful in environmental problem solving, and actively teach them to teachers and students. Another option is to value the knowledge and skill development that practically and responsively emerges as initially unstructured investigations of locally relevant environmental issues proceed. Since the nature of this emergent working knowledge and skills is a function of a particular environmental issue in a particular place and time, its character cannot be foreseen. Such knowledge and skills refer for their authority not to traditional disciplines, but to the environmental issue of the time.

One conclusion from the Environmental Education and Computer Conference project was that in environmental problem solving, the curriculum is an action-based, community-embedded form of inquiry. It yields working knowledge that indicates what changes are required in the dimensions of education theory, teaching method, research, teacher support, materials, and overall project design (Greenall Gough & Robottom, 1993). The project demonstrated that two of the mainstays of traditional curriculum—a universal course content and textbooks as the prime source of knowledge—are inapplicable in environmental problem solving.

A third, related issue concerns the applied science interest in generalizability. There is a tendency in the model/module approach to environmental problem solving to be bedazzled by certain scientific qualities. Yet the most compelling examples of environmental problem solving are those where collaborative groups of teachers, students, and members of various community agencies have worked together to resolve a local environmental issue. The curriculum outcomes of such collaborative work tend to be nongeneralizable. The nature of the problem, its solution, and the knowledge and skills developed in that resolution were idiosyncratic. The value lay in their authenticity.

Conclusion

We need to shift the way we conceive our task in the field of environmental problem solving away from a models/modules approach toward a more responsive, collaborative, critical and community-based form of curriculum reconstruction. To summarize this shift, I reproduce a table from O'Donoghue & McNaught (1991) that is transactional rather than transmissional, generative and emergent rather than pre-determined, opportunistic rather than systematic, and idiosyncratic rather than generalizable (Figure 2:9). The challenges involved in working through these shifts represent the environmental education research agenda for the decade of the nineties.

FIGURE 2:9
*Initial Rational
Framework /
Revised Political
Economy*

Initial Rational Framework	Revised Political Economy
1. Educational Theory (Pedogogy)	
A positivist orientation compatible with the determinism of behaviorist theories and fundamental pedagogies.	An interpretive position illuminated by an eclectic synthesis of symbolic interactionism, phenomenology, constructivist science, and critical theory.
2. Teaching Method (Didactics)	
Structured study guides and techniques for fieldwork experiences that both inculcate the scientific method and develop a hierarchy of scientific process skills.	Experiential learning and dialogic interaction in inquiry and problem solving settings that have been developed through a process of negotiation with the pupils.
3. Research/Evaluation	
A disciplined and systematic process of problem identification, research, resource development, pilot testing (evaluation as measurement), and dissemination.	Action research and sustained support to facilitate teacher resource development and problem solving through a contextual critical process of praxis (evaluation as a critical process driving change).
4. Workshop Style	
On-off demonstrations, lectures, and contrived situations at centers away from schools.	Sustained discussion, problem defining, and resource development with teacher working groups in schools and at field centers.
5. Resource Materials	
Expert written, field tested, and packaged materials and activities to be used by teachers in predetermined ways.	An expanding pool of materials and techniques written by teachers or adapted to local needs by curriculum projects.
6. Project Design	
The Action Ecology kit of resource materials and activities for an ecology fieldwork.	A pool of resources for an environmental education support service.

References

AJEE. (1991). Contemporary issues forum: A national curriculum for environmental education? *Australian Journal of Environmental Education* 7: 88–116.

Armstrong, S. (1991). An uphill battle ... Downstream. *Explorer* 2: 21–23.

Bird, G. (1990). Water quality testing. Report of the activities of Lorne HES. In Muhlebach & Robottom (1990) *Environmental education and computer conferences project: Supporting community-based environmental education.* Geelong, Victoria: Deakin Institute for Studies on Education.

Elliott, J. (1991). Developing community-focussed environmental education through action research. Draft paper tabled at an OECD seminar on "Participatory research and environmental education." Orwich, England: The University of East Anglia, 21–28 June.

Greenall Gough, A. & Robottom, I. (1993). Towards a socially critical environmental education: Water quality studies in a coastal school. *Journal of Curriculum Studies* 25(2).

Muhlebach, R. & Robottom, I. (1990). *Environmental education and computer conferences project: Supporting community-based environmental education.* Geelong, Victoria: Deakin Institute for Studies on Education.

O'Donoghue, R. & McNaught, C. (1991). Environmental education: The development of a curriculum through 'grass-roots' reconstructive action. *International Journal of Science Education* 13(4): 391–404.

Papagiannis, G.; Kless, S.; & Bickel, R. (1982). Towards a political economy of educational innovation. *Review of Educational Research* 52(2): 245–290.

Popkewitz, T. (1984). *Paradigm and ideology in educational research.* London: Falmer Press.

Posch P. (1988). The project "Environment and School Initiatives." In OECD (1988) *Environment and school initiatives*: International Conference, Linz, September 1988. Paris: OECD.

Robottom, I. (1987). Two paradigms of professional development in environmental education. *The Environmentalist* 7(4): 291–298.

Robottom, I. (1991). Matching the purposes of environmental education with consistent approaches to research and professional development. Gold Coast, Queensland: National Conference of the Australian Association for Research in Education, 29 November.

Robottom, I. & Hart, P. (1990). Computer conferences in environmental education: can they help to transcend the division of labor in EE? In Rohwedder, R. (ed.) *Computer-aided environmental education.* Troy, Ohio: NAAEE.

Robottom, I. & Muhlebach, R. (1989). Expanding the scientific community in schools: a community conference in science education. *Australian Science Teachers Journal* 35(1): 39–47.

Shepherd, J. & Norman, P. (1990). Marine Science/Biology. Report on the activities of Queenscliff Secondary College. In Muhlebach, R. & Robottom, I. (1990). *Environmental education and computer conferences project: Supporting community-based environmental education.* Geelong, Victoria: Deakin Institute for Studies on Education..

Wills, B. (1990). Communications, science and the environment. Report on the activities of Warrnambool Secondary College. In Muhlebach, R. & Robottom, I. (1990). *Environmental education and computer conferences project: Supporting community-based environmental education.* Geelong, Victoria: Deakin Institute for Studies on Education.

Wood, D. (1990). Environment action at Irymple South. *Connect* 66: 5–15.

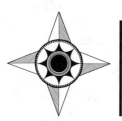

MODELS AND APPROACHES : PART 5
A Brief Analysis

MARGARET T. TUDOR

What's Similar?

The four approaches presented here have much in common. Certainly, they share a lofty goal in their aim to empower learners to interact effectively and democratically in their own communities. While the approaches differ, all of them provide opportunities for students to model an investigative problem solving process, which ideally helps prepare the learner for a lifetime of effective community problem solving.

All of them assume that while students may develop many problem solving skills earlier, learning the problem solving *process* should begin in middle school. All the approaches stress that providing a real-world context for environmental issue problem solving is essential for developing interdisciplinary problem solving skills. All require that students familiarize themselves with local issues, in hopes that they will find something that relates to their educational experience and to their personal lives.

Finally, each approach implies changes within the traditional curriculum to accommodate an interdisciplinary problem solving approach. Each supports innovations such as cross-curriculum and team teaching. Although to different extremes, with all these approaches, teachers are challenged to work on their role as facilitator and model for the learners. Each author recognizes that teachers need their own support base to fulfill that role and suggests ways to build that necessary base.

What's Different?

At the same time, these approaches represent very different assumptions about how structured or preplanned a problem solving effort needs to be, the prerequisites and nature of the "knowledge" one needs to address an environmental problem, and the role of the educator in that process. In terms of all of these parameters, one can fairly systematically place these approaches on a continuum with Hungerford at one extreme, Hammond and Stapp in the middle, and Robottom at the other.

The Level of Structure in the Process
One of the most defining differences among the approaches lies in how much structure overlays the students' experiential learning. Hungerford provides the

most structure with a systematic progression through his investigative program. This approach maintains scientific methodology will lead the investigation to a well-grounded problem definition and, consequently, a logical solution.

Structure in the Stapp and Hammond method varies between relatively structured skill-building activities and more flexible student-based exploration. At the other end of this continuum, Robottom advocates an unstructured problem solving process. He would argue that each issue and, consequently, its investigation will be idiosyncratic and contextual. In addition, creating a structure, from the Robottom perspective, implies a teacher-driven, predetermined goal that does not offer students an opportunity to solve the problem themselves.

**FIGURE 2:10
Comparison of
Problem-Solving
Models**

Hungerford	Hammond/Stapp	Robottom
More structure	<·······························>	Less structure
Investigation before action	<·······························>	Action informs investigation
Teacher as leader	<·······························>	Teacher as co-learner

What Students Need to Know Prior to Taking Action

The Hungerford model assumes students need content knowledge as a prerequisite. Ecological foundations and environmental awareness ideally are developed before sixth grade. When students are older, this understanding helps guide their problem solving process. In terms of the issue investigation itself, Hungerford requires an exhaustive investigation of primary and secondary materials. His approach lays out a sequence of steps for student skill development.

Hammond, Stapp, and Robottom expect some of the issue understanding to come from taking action. They assume that content knowledge and imagery of problem solving are jointly developed during the process of problem solving. Stapp recommends the teacher assess and address the needs for skill building for students before environmental issue problem solving. From Robottom's perspective the teacher does not direct the curriculum through specific skill development. Skills emerge from experiencing the problem solving process and are developed with successive attempts to problem solve.

What This Means for the Teacher

Each author describes strategies for teachers to redefine their roles, ranging from Hungerford's traditional teaching-for-competency style to Hammond's and Stapp's less structured role as facilitator and coach. Robottom challenges educators to be researchers, qualitatively studying and reporting on the process which they and their students undertake. In this context the teacher, by focusing on process, enables students to direct their attention to aspects of the problem as they arise. The teacher facilitates the emerging curriculum generated by the students' investigation and responds to their need to know. The educator is responsible for reflecting on his or her teaching practice and changing it to fit the students' needs. The teacher becomes a learner as well.

Going Beyond The Words: Adapting The Approaches To Your Setting

In all of these approaches, educators provide role models and some kind of leadership in the classroom. They enable the formation of a support structure and offer instruction that helps students see and experience the problem solving process. These four approaches provide guidelines for how teachers can help their students undertake the process. As proven approaches, they span a continuum of possibilities, from structured to less structured, from the planned to the responsive.

Chapter 1 argued that to solve multidisciplinary problems learners need to have a multifaceted understanding of the problem and to be able to make comparisons across their cognitive maps. Ideally, learners will have an opportunity to work with and stretch their understanding. They will be encouraged to shift between levels of understanding and to connect with other perspectives. The specifics of each classroom setting, of course, depend on many factors. It is our hope that educators can adopt or adapt an approach to suit their teaching situation, philosophy, and style; the students' learning needs and styles; and cultural context.

This may involve modifying aspects of each approach to develop a method of your own. For example, one could combine Hungerford's structured approach to scientific methodology with Stapp's group processing, support building strategies. Similarly Hammond's approach may be strengthened by incorporating aspects of Hungerford's skill development. Elements of Hammond's approach such as mentoring and early group development work with Stapp's approach. Considering all three models together, Stapp provides the framework for problem solving into which Hungerford's scientific methodology skills emphasis and Hammond's group organizing techniques dovetail. Robottom advocates another framework or paradigm through which these approaches may be viewed. His approach is complete for the educator wishing to adopt his responsive opportunistic problem-solving process. At the same time, the initial development of a supportive environment and the mentoring proposed in the Stapp and Hammond models are not inconsistent with Robottom's framework. Chapter 3, Practitioners' Voices, offers a sampling of such efforts by other educators to teach problem solving.

What's Missing?

All of these approaches fill many of the requirements for effective problem solving developed in Chapter 1. They all deal with real, local problems in which students contribute to the solution as members of the community. They provide mechanisms for building familiarity with the problem: Hungerford through scientific methodology and logical analysis, and Stapp, Hammond, and Robottom through modeling the process, which allows the process to emerge in response to the problem. They all include an evaluation and assessment phase.

As discussed in Chapter 1, however, the process of defining the problem is perhaps the most crucial aspect of effective problem solving. From a cognitive point of view, interdisciplinary problem solving is best served by a patterned cognitive map from which a problem definition is developed from several perspectives (social, scientific, technological, historical, political, etc.) Taking the time to define a problem means learners stay in the problem space. There, they spend their time comparing across maps, creating linkages and perspectives that enrich their problem understanding and broaden the range of possible solutions.

While all of these approaches can provide students with a setting to understand an issue and develop some problem solving skills, none of them adequately encourages learners to stay in the problem space and develop a problem definition from several perspectives. Hungerford's emphasis on issue investigation comes the closest to meeting this need, while Stapp, Hammond and Robottom put the emphasis on the exploring the solution space instead. Nevertheless, even the Hungerford approach supports a rather speedy and narrow definition of the problem. Without some conscious skill building and emphasis on strategies for staying in the problem space, students will have difficulty framing multidisciplinary problems.

Chapter 4 offers some activities that start to address these cognitive interdisciplinary skills. The exercises encourage development of cognitive maps into multilevel hierarchies with links to other maps, thus producing a richer pattern of knowledge. These skill development activities fit into the Hungerford–Stapp–Hammond paradigms, but will not be appropriate for the Robottom paradigm.

Conclusion

This chapter focused on four well-received, articulate approaches to teaching environmental problem solving. All have reported success in case studies and through research. They have proven themselves workable in both formal and nonformal settings. While they represent a significant start in our efforts to deal with the interdisciplinary character of environmental problem solving, these approaches are only a start. This effort will ultimately depend on the ingenuity and commitment of the educators who use and adapt such approaches. The next chapter is a discussion of some of those efforts.

PRACTITIONER VOICES

MARTHA C. MONROE

The excitement in the air was almost audible as the school bus pulled up to the surface site of Middleborough's water supply, the Pratt Farm wetlands. The fifth graders pouring out of the bus weren't concerned about the mud or the chilly May wind, because this trip culminated a two-month study of wetlands—their wetlands. A great blue heron lifted off from the distant marsh and 20 kids fumbled to lift binoculars to their faces. Those who didn't bother got a better look. "There goes its neck into an 'S'"exclaimed Sonya, keying in on an identifying clue. Her friend agreed, "Just like in the slides!"

The students would spend the field session exploring the wetland and collecting data on the developing problems. Back at school, they would employ the data as the basis for solutions. As in past years, some students would write letters of concern, some would build nest boxes for birds, and others would choose to "get the word out" with a poster or brochure.

from Albright-Burton, "Care for Wetland Birds"

Across the continent, educators are creating and participating in programs aimed at helping learners gain problem solving skills. There are many different programs, even in the realm of environmental education. Some focus on understanding the problem (in Appendix, see Ady, Baugh, Fialkowski). Others, like Albright-Burton, provide learners with opportunities to explore an issue and practice action taking skills (see also Steinbach, Sauvé and Boutard). There are programs that distill the skills and practice them separately (see Kowal), while others provide opportunities for learners to immerse themselves in efforts to address some problem (see Ogle).

This chapter represents the diversity in environmental problem solving programs. This review does not summarize the state of the art in problem solving education. Rather, it provides imagery of the possible by using descriptions of some practical and achievable programs to reinforce several themes of environmental problem solving. Taken together, these descriptions add the voice of experience to the theory and the models of teaching environmental problem solving.

Members of the North American Association for Environmental Education (NAAEE) volunteered descriptions of their successful programs in teaching problem solving. The themes that emerged from these descriptions form the basis of this chapter. While it is not surprising that these themes mirror those developed in the first chapter, it is heartening to see the linkages between theory and practice. From the practitioners' voices, three important characteristics underpin effective problem solving programs:

1. They are relevant to learners.

2. They provide a supportive learning environment.

3. They model the problem solving process, and involve students in that process.

Successful Programs Are Relevant

When asked "What makes your efforts to teach environmental problem solving successful?" most of our respondents said they use problems and exercises *relevant* to the learners. This simple characteristic is essential to the theory of problem solving outlined in Chapter 1. Relevant issues touch on something the learners already know, something tangible, or something they care about or find interesting. Starting with the familiar or with some method for learners to connect to what they know can greatly facilitate their efforts to build an understanding or "cognitive map" of the problem.

The discussion in Chapter 1 also suggests learners who see some relevance to the issues are likely to solve problems better. They are more likely to spend time in the problem-framing and problem solving space, and less inclined to "jump to solutions." It is the richness of their cognitive map that enables them to explore other solutions even after arriving at one answer. As one might expect, our practitioners found several different ways to focus on a topic of relevance.

They Can See It
Much of students' classroom learning is fairly abstract—they talk and read about issues, but rarely *do* anything about them. It takes great effort to make learning concrete and real. Several of the educators contributing to this monograph felt that having students see the environmental issues with their own eyes made lessons seem more relevant. They often used field trips as opportunities for learners to see the sources of some of their environmental concerns. For example, Carol Fialkowski of the Chicago Academy of Sciences helps Chicago teachers understand some environmental solutions by having them visit a coal-burning utility plant, a restored prairie, and a methane-reclaiming landfill. Since the focus of these courses is on problems and their solutions rather than simply content knowledge, it is a new approach for most urban teachers.

It is difficult to "see" an issue when it is far away, so eighth grade teacher Alice Steinbach chooses a local issue for students to investigate. She notes that "This lends relevance and also involves parents." Using aerial photographs, local speakers, and field trips to the site, students gather firsthand knowledge of the problem, information that would not be available were the issue not in their backyard.

Dan Kowal, coordinator of the Logan School's Environmental Education program in Denver, Colorado, takes students "to the source of what they are studying, inspiring the students' interest in environmental affairs and offering opportunities for observation, interpretation, analysis, synthesis, and evaluation: skill areas that are crucial to problem solving." Field trips to reservoirs, lumber mills, and power plants teach his students about the complexity of environmental issues.

They Can Study It and Make Linkages to Their Lives

A non-local issue can be relevant if it touches on the learner's life. Some teachers help students explore the issues and understand the connections to themselves. To do so, many programs have students collect and use data to formulate their understanding of the issues. This information may support their claims about the severity of the problem or of the benefits of a solution. The students become experts, fueled with hard facts to back the fervor of their conviction.

From a cognitive perspective, having students ask their own questions, rather than those posed by the teacher, facilitates cognitive map building in two ways. First, the process of asking questions keeps learners off the "solution" phase. Second, having the learners address their own questions helps them build maps that connect to and expand on what they already know. Such maps represent better understanding. Therefore, problem solving programs that guide students through a data collection and questioning phase encourage them to build a map of the problem space. This is Step 1 of the problem solving process described in Chapter 1.

Ivan Baugh's curriculum in Louisville, Kentucky uses computer technology to help in the analysis and comparison of the data students collect. One of his units compares the quantity of garbage generated in the community to the space needed to accommodate it at a landfill. The issue is extremely relevant when students use a computer spreadsheet to determine the amount of garbage their school generates based on their classroom output. Students can "see" the benefits of recycling from a HyperCard simulation that peels recyclables out of the waste stream. When the class combines all the data, the impact is significant.

In Middleborough, Massachusetts, fifth graders, teachers, scientists, and community volunteers worked together to protect the wetlands that supply the town with fresh water. The program, developed by the Manomet Bird Observatory (MBO), allowed teachers to incorporate local environmental issues into their "Texas-based" science texts. Research staff at MBO supplied teachers with local data and relevant activities both of which helped children develop a sense of responsibility for something they "owned"—their own community. The steady decline of specific wetland birds in Massachusetts, for example, correlated well to habitat degradation.

Scientific data were the cornerstone of another problem solving effort where the population decline of four species of migratory geese prompted the U.S. Fish and Wildlife Service (USFWS) to design an Information and Education program to accompany their management plan. The task force, working closely with Native Alaskans, created a myriad of products and programs to inform residents of the Pacific Flyway about the plan. A calendar art contest, a comic book, visits to the community and schools by native USFWS staff, and a school curriculum program called "Teach About Geese" helped create awareness, provide information, and alter the norm of harvesting geese. Here, too, the information about the problem and the potential solutions were of greatest interest to people who live with the geese.

Not all connections are easy to see. Students' skills or attitudes may need improvement before the relevance is clear. Well-designed discussions can help students make the connections between the skills they learned, the information they gathered, and the problems they see around them. Anne Camozzi of Antigonish, Nova Scotia, found a simple exercise called Hollow Squares (Pfeiffer & Jones, 1974, and Common Squares, Chapter 4) helps students practice the skills they need to work effectively together—the ability to communicate, listen, and think creatively. She noticed that when a local environmental issue is introduced and students are asked to brainstorm solutions using these skills, students generate energy and excitement as they think and work together.

They Choose It

Incorporating student choice into problem solving is another mechanism for designing a program that will be relevant to the learners. It is a simple strategy for identifying a topic in which the learners are interested. At the same time, it presents a fair number of challenges as well. The act of choosing is empowering, but it takes tremendous skill to organize and manage the effort so students select projects at a level fitting the academic time frame, matching their skills, and promising some modicum of success and feedback.

Choosing a problem, a solution, or an action requires that learners practice elements of the problem solving process. In all of these cases, the students need to explore both the problem and the solution space as they compare their skills and resources to the needs of the issue. Several activities in Chapter 4 demonstrate these skills. There is more, however, to making a "good" choice. A good choice engages the affective components of interest, motivation, and personal investment.

Lucie Sauvé and Armel Boutard from Quebec recognize these benefits and challenges, and report excellent results in their university course.

"We consider that the success of the Environmental Problem Solving course can be attributed (in part) to the students' personal involvement in solving a problem of their choice. This contributed to their great motivation and the development of a feeling of responsibility toward its resolution. They felt satisfied by working on a real problem, by becoming specialists on that problem, and by being socially helpful. Most accepted working more hours than the number suggested. An

atmosphere of enthusiasm and happiness prevailed during the final presentations as further testimony to the great interest of the students."

Eighth grade students in Alice Steinbach's class did not choose which issue they explored (she selects a local issue), but decided how they would take action. Again, Steinbach provides adequate structure and guidance.

> *"Each student, either individually or in small groups, worked on an independent project chosen with consideration for his or her interests, talents, and abilities. These activities included letters to government officials and editors of local newspapers, posters urging community members to recycle and eliminate unnecessary solid and toxic wastes, stories about solid and toxic waste concerns for children, political cartoons, and using nontoxic alternative cleansers at home.... By allowing students to choose among a variety of ways to get involved, the success rate of students ranged between 85 and 95% on most activities, and participation was near 100%."*

In the ultimate demonstration of "choice" represented by these examples, the Puget Sound Water Quality Authority gave citizen groups an opportunity to determine how they wanted to affect water quality concerns in their region. It then funded the proposed efforts from the Public Involvement and Education (PIE) Fund. The program is based on several assumptions central to the theory of problem solving, such as having the learner identify the problems and issues. Robert Steelquist relates one example:

> *Pacific Iron and Metal, a Seattle scrap metal recycler, discovered that in spite of a strong corporate policy of being environmentally friendly, management practices in their scrapyard contributed to high levels of stormwater contamination following major rainstorms. Investigating their own problems, they found a wide range of inexpensive "best management practices" (BMP's) that would reduce stormwater pollution. In their PIE Fund project, Pacific Iron and Metal developed a BMP handbook and a series of workshops for others in the scrap recycling industry — including their competitors. The peer education program has attracted the attention of a national trade organization which hopes to adopt the method for other scrap recyclers as a way of identifying and correcting stormwater problems within the industry. The lesson: learners can identify significant problems with water quality; many can assist in the solution if provided the resources.*

At Swarthmore College, student choice shaped the entire learning experience in Peter Blaze Corcoran's environmental education course. Students like Eric Sievers helped select discussion topics, speakers, and class readings. It may have taken additional class time, but the students reveled in role playing the diverse perspectives on nature they chose: an Oregon lumberjack, an urban child, a Third World woman gathering wood, and a human virus. Their participation in the specifics of the course made it relevant to their lives, interests, and experiences.

In general, previous experience and knowledge will greatly affect the learners' ability to choose a reasonable project. Of these examples, only adult learners had total discretion. How much choice can younger learners handle? What exposure to the issue must they have before making a choice? Much of this decision depends on their familiarity with the problem, i.e., the extent of their cognitive map and the thoroughness with which they attended to Step 1 of problem solving—exploring the problem space.

Successful Programs Provide a Supportive Learning Environment

Problem solving takes experimentation, creativity, flexibility, risk taking, and independent thinking. Those qualities tend to arise in environments where student differences are respected, individuals honored, and failure allowed. Such is a supportive environment—supportive and nurturing of the qualities that enhance problem solving skills. This environment may be designed by the educator, created by the richness of information and resources available, or developed within the learning community. Several practitioners spoke about the importance of this kind of environment and described several different versions.

The Supportive Environment

Many contributors commented on the importance of a supportive, or "exploratory," environment as we called it in Chapter 1. Michael Cohen of Project NatureConnect suggests that we have access to a most supportive environment, Nature. We need to build the sensitivities to recognize it. "Motivated people solve problems.... Without being bonded to the natural environment, we are not motivated to act on its behalf."

Other contributors relied more on the dynamics of the teaching setting itself to create support. For Peter Blaze Corcoran and Eric Sievers, such a setting is the heart of their environmental education course. "The development of a close community in the classroom encouraged emotional expression as well as intellectual exploration, allowing students to express despair over the ecological crisis as well as hope for the resolution of environmental problems."

The environment may become supportive with the provision of information. Janis Albright-Burton at Manomet believes informed teachers feel more confident about their abilities to participate in environmental programs and try something new. The MBO research staff provide an appropriate scientific background through a teacher training workshop, and the teachers return to the classroom to help students wrestle with solving watershed problems.

Alice Steinbach sees a supportive environment as one in which students realize success, and since her students' cognitive skills range from elementary to college level, she adapts the assignment to enable students to use their different talents. She balances students' needs and her own constraints of time and resources by creating a variety of activities and involvements in the assignment to allow students to experience success. Her role is critical to help gauge the problem and solution so that the students are likely to achieve.

In a supportive environment, learners often receive helpful feedback. In Alice Steinbach's class, this extends beyond the classroom experience to include community recognition and responses from governmental officials. In the PIE Fund, feedback comes through improved environmental quality. The PIE Fund projects must define their goals with measurable indicators—an ongoing challenge to the contractors. One project focused on non-point pollution within a watershed using a decrease in nitrogen levels in the stream as the feedback mechanism. After storm-drain stenciling, the production of a homeowner's guide to the watershed, and classroom programming in schools, levels of nitrogen in the stream declined measurably. Although environmental feedback such as this indicates the problem is being solved, not that the people are learning problem solving skills, it certainly supports the atmosphere for successful problem solving and experimentation.

Teaching Skills of Group Support and Leadership

Environmental issues are rarely solved by one individual. They require the cooperation and input of a number of interests and perspectives. The soundness of our solutions depends in part on the effectiveness of our ability to work together. How well a group can accomplish Step 2 in the problem solving process, exploring and expanding ways of seeing the problem and solution, is critical to that ability. Whether it entails learning how to run a meeting, to work with a small team, to collaborate with a former adversary, or to acknowledge people's different learning styles and values, each example below represents a strategy for accomplishing a greater understanding of how to view a problem.

The skills required for effective team work and collaboration, however, are not intuitive or natural. Practitioners recognize that leadership skills and the ability to work in a small group must be cultivated and supported. The experiential environmental education program at the Logan School uses skill-building activities as one of several avenues to encourage the development of certain problem solving skills:

> *The environmental education (E.E.) program emphasizes group building and leadership exercises to strengthen the group process skills of each individual. Some field trips are solely dedicated to developing these skills. Throughout many field studies, the facilitator relates individual and group initiatives to solving problems in the participants' lives. By translating leadership and cooperative behaviors from these experiences to those needed in solving real environmental issues, the E.E. program works to build the self-confidence and self-esteem individuals need to meet the challenges ahead of them.*

Lucie Sauvé and Armel Boutard mention the same concerns in their year-long program in Environmental Studies. There, students experience problem solving by tackling a local community problem in small groups. One key element to the success of the course is that students work together, creating a synergy that supports ongoing teamwork.

Anne Camozzi uses the activity Hollow Squares to help learners gain skills in group dynamics and problem solving. The game starts discussion and quickly moves the classroom dynamics to support the development of problem solving skills. This activity works because it is challenging, fun, and the students are totally responsible for the outcome. Cooperation is one of the skills that the game employs. Student observers are quick to notice when the group does or does not work together well, the outcome of which is often success or failure.

As Ruth Jacquot at Murray State University in Kentucky points out, recognizing that people have different learning styles and ways of thinking is an important problem solving strategy. Like the group process skills, working with other learning styles is not intuitive.

> *Knowledge of our own learning style and the style of the other participants in the process is an aid to the process of problem solving. Learners who know themselves and how they work best, who can find out how the participants in the process prefer to work and how they are most successful, can focus on that successful process and aim at reaching consensus (Kolb, 1984). We can develop empathy for different points of view and different processes of problem solving and learning by approaching them without judgment and with respect for individual differences.*

The PIE Fund also encourages a problem solving process that brings participants face to face with different perspectives. The funding requirements were designed to help some of the project's leaders learn skills in listening, negotiating, and problem solving. Each project must select an Advisory Board, preferably with representation from all those who have a stake in the problem. As a result, some boards contain traditionally opposed viewpoints that must be reconciled so the programs develop. The PIE Fund encourages people to move beyond the "us and them" mentality by forcing "odd couples" to design and carry out the PIE Fund project together.

Community Support

A supportive environment can go beyond the classroom or board table. In the following two examples, the problem solving efforts of the participants are linked with and encouraged by the larger community. An important element in the success of Manomet's wetlands program was its effort to address a genuine need in the town. As a result, it drew active community support. Town volunteers participated in the teacher workshops and helped teach during the field sessions. Parents were active volunteers throughout the project. Newspapers carried the story, and the library developed a list of important wetland reference books for children and adults.

The combination of programs and materials supplied to the Alaskans of the Yukon-Kuskokwin Delta about their geese populations was so well designed that it supported a new concept of goose utilization. People who had collected eggs and goslings for years were beginning to understand the impact of their harvest and to believe that they should not do so. An evaluation of the program revealed a simple but powerful example of this changing norm: the family of the winner of the art contest decided not to catch goslings and comfortably reported this decision to their peers in a high school classroom. The community supported a new way of thinking about the environment and problem solving.

Re-creating community is the cornerstone of a project three different institutions co-sponsored in Arlington, Virginia. The Potomac Overlook Nature Center, the Mt. Olivet United Methodist Church, and the Sullivan House (a transitional housing unit) joined forces to support interns who spearheaded recycling drives, a summer concert series, helped with transportation and child care, and landscaped the three locations. Martin Ogle explains:

> *The cooperative project has been valuable in that it built a stronger sense of community among the three organizations and fostered relationships between the people in them. Since the project is set in the context of society which is extremely specialized and which measures its success on ever-increasing consumption rates, it sometimes seems we are a lonely voice with limited outreach. Yet the project has concrete results: The activities have helped people; the project has changed people's outlook on life, and we have dealt with difficult problems head-on.*

Successful Programs Involve Learners in the Problem Solving Process

One of the most important points made in Chapter 1 is that competent problem solving takes a combination of skills, knowledge, and experience. The notion of cognitive apprenticeship and learner involvement mentioned there recur throughout these examples. These educators recognize that students learn skills best when they practice, discuss, and reflect on them. They have adapted their programs accordingly. Educators use different strategies, but all feel that with practice students gain the confidence they need to take on the "real world"—the process of practicing problem solving is empowering.

Citizen participation is at the core of the PIE Fund Program at the Puget Sound Water Quality Authority. The program exists to provide a support structure for citizens to participate actively in solving environmental problems. The PIE Fund assumes that citizens and organizations can solve many of Puget Sound's problems, given assistance and resources. This is a rare example of institutionalized environmental problem solving. By giving citizens the resources to solve problems, the program allows people to learn these skills.

By the same token, the Environmental Issues Forum courses introduces teachers to environmental issues in the manner they will use to introduce such topics to their K-8 students. The courses model the teaching process: first exploring issues and problems, then gaining knowledge and content, and finally understanding solutions and actions. As they observe, compare, contrast, experiment, analyze, and synthesize in the course, the teachers realize that these same techniques can be transferred to the classroom. According to Carol Fialkowski, they begin to say, "Hey, I can do this!"

Ivan Baugh notes that students began to change their environmental behaviors through his technology-based environmental investigation units. The active participation of the students provides ownership and demonstrates how each individual counts. Because students work with personal data (e.g., water usage, garbage generation, automobile use habits, energy use, recycling), they become more committed to change. The development and execution of school-based campaigns for change help students apply their new insights and receive feedback from a real-world audience.

Dan Kowal at the Logan School claims the environmental education program is premised on the belief that problem solving is not accomplished by a formula. He believes it is the creativity behind the solutions that make them work. And that creativity is a product of a thorough and well-balanced study of the problem and of experiencing it firsthand. In addition to exposing students in a variety of environmental issues, perspectives, and potential solutions, the Logan School reinforces the mental flexibility needed to creatively see solutions by incorporating a phase for critical thinking and reflection. The students process what they learn and apply those concepts to another issue. Kowal remembers,

> *During wrap-up times, students often share how they never considered particular viewpoints until they came on a field trip, or understood the complexity of an issue until they were confronted with it face to face. The students comment favorably on having a strong element of control in all activities. As opposed to just reading about an environmental problem in a book or being lectured to, students enjoy the flexibility to examine the situation firsthand and having the latitude to solve things on their own.*

Concluding Comments

The themes suggested here bind together a marvelously diverse set of approaches to teaching environmental problem solving. Clearly, there is no one right way. Nor do all these contributors agree on what elements are essential. For some, the outdoor experience is powerful; for others, taking action is more important. These examples, like the concepts discussed in Chapter 1, suggest that success of these teaching efforts depends more on how students come to understand and practice the process of problem solving than on a specific activity or piece of information.

For example, several contributors mentioned the value of an outdoor experience to understand the environmental problem better, or to become reconnected to nature. We learned from Chapter 1 that for those experiences to be more than a fun adventure, students need a context for understanding them. Such experiences help learners explore the problem space in greater depth, if students have some familiarity with the issue, if they can see a meaningful connection to their lives, and if they can see how the problem fits into the larger picture of a world they care about.

The themes voiced by these practitioners nicely echo the theoretic base developed in Chapter 1. In summary, they reiterate that to be successful, an effort to teach problem solving needs to:

1. Deal with Issues Relevant to the Learners
To be relevant the issue has to be a meaningful part of the learners' cognitive map, or to hold that promise. People are less likely to build an understanding about issues they find uninteresting or confusing. Students are more likely to attend to information built on what they already know, information that piques their interest and concern.

2. Happen in Settings that Support Exploration, Tolerate Failure, and Encourage Group Cooperation
Being confused is an uncomfortable cognitive state. Group dynamics and conflict are likewise awkward. The human tendency to jump to some kind of understanding or answer means that many problems are not explored adequately before they are "solved" or "settled." A setting that provides structure and facilitates ways of working through that confusion; one that sorts out the complexities and allows for time to focus on problem definition is essential to good problem solving. The group aspect of this process adds the element of diversity. Students need to learn to listen, cooperate, and value differences.

3. Involve the Learners in the Process of Addressing the Issues and Encourage Choice, a Sense of Responsibility, and Reflection
Humans learn by experience—both direct and vicarious. The opportunity to participate in the problem solving process is critical. As students learn to look for and agree on solutions, they gain the skills to help act on those solutions. To be effective problem solvers, they need to know that solutions are achievable, and they can play a role in their accomplishment.

References

Kolb, D. A. (1984). Problem management: Learning from experience. In Srivastva, S. (ed.) *The executive mind*. San Francisco, CA: Jossey-Bass.

Pfeiffer, J.W. & J.E. Jones (1974). *The handbook of structured experiences for human relations training* (Vol. 2.) San Diego, CA: University Associates.

ACTIVITIES TO HELP DEVELOP PROBLEM SOLVING SKILLS

A consistent thread throughout this monograph is the importance of experience and familiarity in effective problem solving. Another emphasis is on the importance of building skills and providing students with the imagery and knowledge they need to feel ready to tackle a real world problem. These skills can be divided into separate steps that can be practiced in or out of context. This chapter offers some activities that allow students to practice parts of the problem solving process.

One word of caution, however: the research to date indicates that problem solving skills do not transfer easily from one problem to another. Knowing how to identify a ruptured appendix and remove it does not help one identify and replace a faulty carburetor. Should we expect that experience with a committee siting a landfill will help facilitate meetings to change local traffic patterns? To a limited extent, it might be helpful. Skills for finding information, managing a group discussion, or understanding others' positions might transfer to a new problem space. For the most part, however, problem solving skill is founded on knowing a great deal about the specifics of the problem at hand.

Familiarity with each problem seems to be essential for being able to "see" a solution. Hence, the initial steps of mental model building are particularly crucial. However, this step of problem exploration and investigation may not always be the first phase of problem solving; it may occur after an initial action (and likely disappointment) leads learners to believe that more information is necessary.

Several examples of classroom activities are included in this unit to illustrate how an educator could assist learners to practice the cognitive skills that are helpful in solving problems. They are not identified by grade level or subject, since the problem itself would be chosen or shaped around the abilities and interests of learners. Most of these activities could be modified for many different types of problems.

The activities are divided into the problem solving format explained in Chapter 1:

Step 1: Exploring and Defining the Problem
Step 2: Searching for and Identifying Solutions
Step 3: Implementing and Evaluating Actions

Step 1: EXPLORING AND DEFINING THE PROBLEM

Learning more about the problem may happen in several typical ways:

- Sending students to the library for research reports
- Bringing in a guest speaker
- Taking a field trip
- Watching an audiovisual production

The more specific and local the problem, the less students will learn from these traditional means, and the more they need to seek other ways for exploring the problem. In these cases, try the following:

- Analyzing newspaper articles
- Comparing letters to the editor
- Collecting data from the environment
- Surveying the affected group through a questionnaire
- Attending public meetings
- Interviewing involved parties

Many of these practices are very well documented and explained in the manual *Investigating and evaluating environmental issues and actions* by Hungerford, Litherland, Peyton, Ramsey, Tomera, and Volk. It is available through Stipes Publishing, 10-12 Chester Street, Champaign IL 61820.

Collecting information is just one process in the Problem Exploration phase of problem solving. Ultimately, learners must be able to construct a mental model of the problem that includes connections to related information and is flexible enough to allow the problem to be seen from a variety of perspectives. Building connections and understanding perspectives are two skills that can be practiced, or at least emphasized, in the information-collection stage of problem exploration.

There are many ways these skills could be developed—through individual assignments, team reports, group competitions, etc. The following activities were designed to use cooperative strategies. In addition to the topic area they explore, learners also practice taking responsibility, facilitating a group, completing a task, and working together. Activities that focus on developing communication and group skills are also important, and a few are listed here as well. An excellent resource for these classroom tools is the *Human resource development annual set*, produced every year from 1972 by J. W. Pfeiffer & L. Goodstein, or Pfeiffer & J.E. Jones. They are available through Pfeiffer & Company, 8517 Production Avenue, San Diego, CA 92121-2280.

Activity 1: Alternative Perspectives

Purpose: To consider an issue from various perspectives.
To share information that a group has collected.

Roles*: Facilitator, Recorder, Timekeeper, Prober

Activity:

    a.   In groups, choose roles and make sure they are understood by all.

    b.   Each person answers a series of questions about the issue from their perspective:

        • What are some of the major problems that underlie this issue?
        • What is one particular perspective on this issue?
        • What action would be most beneficial to solve this problem?

    c.   Before the next person shares his or her perspective, he or she first summarizes the previous speaker's comments.

    d.   As a full group, discuss how the individual perspectives were similar and different. How might the problem statement be modified to reflect all of these perspectives?

Comment: This is most helpful when each person will contribute something different and the goal is to make sure that everyone hears and understands the various perspectives. By asking each person to repeat the previous comments, group members are forced to listen very closely to the speaker and compare their own ideas to what is being said.

*Role definitions are listed on page 122.

Reprinted with permission of Linda Lambert, California State University, Hayward, from "Alternative Perspectives," Education Development Center, 1992.

Activity 2: Moral Dilemma

Purpose: To engage learners in an interesting, concrete discussion about a
              moral decision.

Roles*:   Large group facilitator and if desired, small group facilitator,
              Recorder, Timekeeper

Activity:

a.   A moral dilemma is presented to the learners. The dilemma re-
      volves around one character and ends in a "should" question. The
      question involves a moral decision—valuing family or job, environ-
      ment or public health, authority or personal value, convenience or
      safety, nationalism or community, etc.

b.   After a show of hands to indicate how the character should choose,
      the group is divided into small groups each representing various
      perspectives. Each small group discusses prepared questions that
      draw the moral questions out of the dilemma:

      • What should X do?
      • Who will suffer the most if X does this?
      • What are the consequences of this action?
      • What are the alternative choices? consequences?
      • If the roles were changed, how should X behave?
      • What information is missing to make a decision?

Example:

Coal From "Mother Earth"

*Because of the extreme shortages of natural gas and oil, the Southern Electric Company is
considering switching over to cheaper and more plentiful coal as its energy source for
producing electricity. A huge deposit of coal that can be easily and inexpensively strip-
mined is located on a nearby Indian reservation. If the electric company could gain access to
the Indian-owned coal, it could save huge sums of money over what it would normally cost
to extract and transport coal from other locations.*

*The electric company offered the tribal leaders $20 million to lease the land for a period of
10 years. During that time, the electric company would have the right to mine the coal in
the area. Although the Indians really don't want to see their land mined, the money would
help to provide much needed schools, hospitals, and perhaps even jobs for the people on the
reservation.*

The contracts for the 10-year lease contained a reclamation clause, which required the electric company to replant trees and vegetation at the strip-mining site. Jane Denison, a young lawyer for the electric company, has carefully researched the reclamation problem. She learned that replanting this strip-mined area would be unsuccessful. The strip-mining operation would remove all the topsoil and leave mainly infertile soil and rock in its place. In addition, because the land is so steep it could very easily be worn away. In short, the earth would be left bare and useless.

Jane understands the Indians' feelings toward their "Mother Earth." She agrees that their sacred land will be ruined forever. Should Jane inform the Indians about the information she obtained? Why or why not?

Discussion Questions:
- Jane is obviously being bothered by her conscience. (a) What is the "conscientious" action for her to take? (b) Why should it be important for her to follow her conscience? (c) Should one act on one's conscience even if it means breaking an agreement or law?

- Since Jane is working for the electric company, should her responsibility and loyalty to the company come first? Why or why not?

- Some people hold to the idea expressed by the Latin phrase, "caveat emptor," meaning "let the buyer beware." Since Jane's job is to represent the company, should she leave it up to the Indians to "beware" of what they are getting into? Why or why not?

- Assuming that the electric company knows the reclamation program is likely to be ineffective, is it right for it to sign the contract as it is written? Why or why not?

- The Indians will be receiving a large sum of money from the coal mining lease. Shouldn't that be fair enough exchange for any disturbance resulting from the mining operation? Why or why not?

- Do the Indians have any obligations to help provide the country with coal? We are in the middle of an energy crisis. Shouldn't we develop whatever energy sources that are available to us? Why or why not?

- The Indians believe that man and nature are all one spirit. Would doing harm to the Indian land be in effect doing harm to the Indians? Why or why not?

- We will all benefit from the electricity produced from coal. Should the Indians' feelings about the sacred nature of land prevent us from removing coal from the ground? Why or why not?

*Role definitions are listed on page 122.

Reprinted with permission from: Iozzi, L.A., Cheu, J., Harding, W., & Brzenski, N. (1980) Preparing for tomorrow's world, environmental dilemmas: Critical decisions for society. Longmont, CO: Sopris West.

Activity 3: Jigsaw

Purpose: To engage each person in sharing information and contributing to its incorporation into the overall picture.

Roles*:   Each person plays two roles, one in an "expert" group and one in a mixed group.

Activity:

a.   This is a common technique in cooperative-learning manuals. Divide the group into small groups of experts. Each group is the same size. Each group has a task or information to collect. Each group discusses its information so that each person in the group is an expert and is able to independently represent the information.

b.   Groups are reconfigured so one expert from each previous group is in each new group (see Figure 4:1).

c.   Each person (now an expert) explains his/her information to the mixed group and takes notes on every other presentation.

d.   An optional extension is to ask expert groups to reconvene to share the information they learned in their mixed groups.

FIGURE 4:1
Graphic
description of
jigsaw groups

Expert Groups (to learn and prepare)		Mixed Groups (to share)		Expert Groups (to review)	
AA			AB	AA	
A A	BB	AB	C	AA	BB
	BB	C	AB		BB
CC		AB	C	CC	
CC			C	CC	

*Role definitions are listed on page 122.

This activity has been produced in many forms in a variety of educational publications.

Activity 4: Clarifying the Problem

Purpose: The initial understanding of the problem often leads to an exploration that changes the students' concept of what the problem really is. The following set of questions may help guide group discussion to reevaluate and refocus the problem.

Discussion Questions:

- The general problem we have chosen to investigate is . . .

- Some questions we are most interested in and concerned about are . . .

- We have decided that the best statement of the problem we will investigate is . . .

- What information about the science, history, cultures, potential inequities and technology related to this problem do we need to collect? What are the consequences of this problem for each of these areas?

- What issues are involved with this problem?

- What values are involved with these issues and which values are in conflict?

Activity 5: Checking Assumptions and Values

Purpose: How we define a problem, what we consider to be a solution, and whether or not we really understand those who feel differently is sometimes a product of the assumptions and values through which we see the world. A set of statements that reflect the issue the group is studying may be helpful in starting a discussion about those assumptions. The following list is an example of common assumptions that are often at the heart of disagreements about environmental issues and their solutions.

Activity:

a.   Distribute a list of statements to each student and ask them to evaluate if this statement is always true, sometimes true, or always false. They should identify an example that supports their decision.

b. In small groups ask students to discuss their decisions and identify those on which they initially disagree. Ask them to consider how they think other people would react to these statements.

c. Return to a large group and use the following discussion questions to help students understand the impact of these assumptions.

Statements:

a. All growth is good and possible. There are no effective limits to growth.

b. There is an "away." When we throw things "away" they are gone.

c. Technology can solve any problem.

d. New is better than old. Fast is better than slow.

e. Possession of things is the source of happiness.

f. The marketplace determines good and bad products. If it sells, it is good.

g. Consumers are very intelligent. People will buy only what they want.

h. Rational powers of human beings are superior to intuitive or moral powers.

i. Improvements come through more and better technology.

Discussion Questions:

- What group of people tend to believe this statement?

- How does this belief affect their actions?

- How do their actions affect the issue we are studying?

- What might change their mind?

- What is a good example of this statement being false?

- Is it ever true?

Adapted with permission from Meadows, D. (1991) The global citizen. Washington, D.C.: Island Press.

Activity 6: Common Squares

Note: Many students need practice and assistance in moving from a competitive, teacher-has-the-answer, take-a-test mentality to one of problem solving, solution testing, and group work. This activity and the next suggest ways to engage groups in communication and some activities to make evident the skills that are needed.

Purpose: To develop the ability to analyze resources.
To develop the ability to define a problem.
To develop the ability to work in a group.

Activity:

a. Divide the class into groups of 5.

b. Distribute a set of 5 envelopes to each group; each person gets 1 envelope. In each envelope are several shapes (see design), the sum total of which will form 5 squares.

c. Provide the following instructions:
   • There is to be no verbal communication.
   • No one may take a piece belonging to anyone else.
   • Each person is to empty the envelope and place the shapes in front of him/herself.
   • The exercise is completed when each member of the group has an equal-sized, completed square in front of him/herself.

Discussion Questions:
   • Who assumed leadership in the group?

   • Who was giving help and solving the problem?

   • Did you accept help from other group members?

   • Did you sense any signs of sexism in the group?

   • Did you sense any signs of racism in the group?

   • Was there group communication?

   • Was there a total group effort to solve the problem?

   • Were you aware of others' resources?

   • At what point did you feel good about the activity?

Materials: Squares and envelopes

Reprinted with permission from Stapp, W. B. & Cox, D. A. (1979) Environmental education activities manual. Dexter, MI: Thomson-Shore.

Common Square Patterns

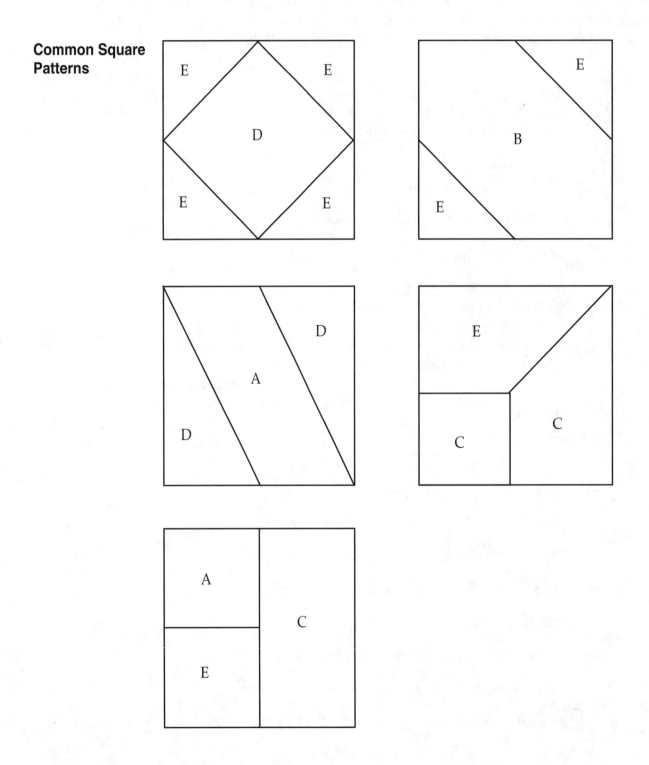

Activity 7: Six Bits

Purpose: To develop the ability to work in a group.
To equally divide critical resources.
To listen with comprehension.
To develop leadership skills.
To organize and analyze data.

Materials:

Choose a solvable problem (preferably with one right answer) with lots of bits of information. Make a set of six cards, each card having directions and information on it, for each group of six students. See sample cards.

Activity:

a. Divide the class into groups of six.

b. Give each group a set of six cards. Each card is different, but each set is identical. Each group member receives one card from the group's set.

c. Inform the groups that one card asks a question; their task is to answer the question.

d. Remind the group members that they cannot show their card to anyone else.

Discussion Questions:

• How did leadership unfold during the exercise?

• How were decisions made?

• How effectively did the group function?

• What made the groups different?

• How might the groups have functioned more effectively?

"I'm Thirsty," adapted with permission from Project WILD. Copyright 1983, 1985, 1992 Western Regional Environmental Education Council (5430 Grosvenor Ln, Bethesda, MD 20814. Phone: 301-493-5447) and from Stapp, W. B. & Cox, D. A. (1979) Environmental education activities manual, Dexter, MI: Thompson Shore.

Sample Cards for Activity 7

Card 1   *You may not show this card to anyone in your group. You may read the information on the card to anyone in the group. Some of the information may be irrelevant.*

The desert bighorn are large, wild sheep that live in the sparsely vegetated areas of the Southwest.

Ewes drink about 1 gallon of water when they visit the waterhole.

Four lambs were killed by predators before summer.

Card 2   *You may not show this card to anyone in your group. You may read the information on the card to anyone in the group. Some of the information may be irrelevant.*

During the hottest months of the summer, ewes and lambs come to the waterhole daily.

What weekly inflow rate is necessary into the waterhole for the population to survive the summer?

All of the ewes that overwintered with the herd are still alive.

Card 3   *You may not show this card to anyone in your group. You may read the information on the card to anyone in the group. Some of the information may be irrelevant.*

Temperatures in the Southwest desert in the summer are frequently over 100 degrees Farenheit.

Ewes are adult female sheep.

Lambs drink 2 pints of water when they visit the waterhole.

Card 4   *You may not show this card to anyone in your group. You may read the information on the card to anyone in the group. Some of the information may be irrelevant.*

During the hottest months of summer, rams (male sheep) may only visit the waterhole once a week.

Last fall this population of desert bighorn had 7 rams and 16 ewes.

For these calculations, assume no other animals or plants use this waterhole.

Card 5   *You may not show this card to anyone in your group. You may read the information on the card to anyone in the group. Some of the information may be irrelevant.*

Rams may range 20 miles away from the waterhole during their wandering.

This waterhole is fed by a spring.

One ram died over the winter.

Card 6   *You may not show this card to anyone in your group. You may read the information on the card to anyone in the group. Some of the information may be irrelevant.*

Rams drink about 4 gallons of water when they come to the waterhole.

The rate of evaporation from the waterhole is 10 gallons a day during the summer.

All of the ewes delivered one healthy lamb each spring.

Step 2: SEARCHING FOR AND IDENTIFYING SOLUTIONS

Many of the models and examples in this monograph gloss over the actual problem solving step. We all too often assume that once we have information, the solution will be obvious. On the contrary, good solutions take work. They take moving through the problem and solution space with proposals and scenarios. They require full use of the flexible model built during the problem identification step and a practical understanding of the solutions. What is likely to work? Who can make it work? Who can prevent it from working? What other interests do those parties bring?

The activities in Step 2 include strategizing about the phase of action taking (Step 3) before the action is ever decided. Much of it occurs in the "what if" mode of thought. For that reason, Step 2 skills are often difficult to pin down. Our tendency to leap to a solution means we spend very little conscious energy on exploring solutions. But if we leap to an unworkable solution, only to discover another problem after we are in Step 3, we will eventually come back to Step 2, enriched by that experience, to explore the solution space again.

The following activities help learners explore solution spaces without committing to a final decision. Different groups may choose different actions; activity results can be compared. Depending upon the group and the problem, one activity may be more appropriate than another.

Activity 8: Cross Impact Matrix

Purpose: To provide a framework for considering how goals, developments, and events may affect each other.
To develop the ability to work in teams.
To encourage learners to consider new problems that arise when old problems are solved.
To help clarify assumptions and reveal inconsistencies in thinking.

Roles* Facilitator, Recorder, Timekeeper, Process Observer

Activity:

a. Ask students to identify 2 to 4 factors that have an impact on their problem.

b. Organize these factors in a matrix for the class.

c. In small groups, ask students to choose roles and then complete the boxes with the impact of one factor on the other. See Figure 4:2.

Discussion Questions:

- Does each impact have both positive and negative implications?

- Which impacts are largely unknown?

- Is it important to explore some of these impacts before we choose a solution?

- What other factors should be considered in a similar matrix?

*Role definitions are listed on page 122.

Adapted with permission from the National Council for the Social Studies from Fitch & Svengalis (1970) Futures unlimited. Washington DC: NCSS.

Figure 4:2 Cross Impact Matrix

	Price of Commercial Vegetables	Price of Organic Vegetables	Availability
Price of Commercial Vegetables	X	Acts as ceiling on price structure for similar products	Lowers when available, due to transportation costs
Price of Organic Vegetables	Reduces the amount of organic material sold because price is lower and more available	X	Lowers when in season
Availability	In all stores and markets for reasonable prices	In speciality stores, co-ops and markets	X

- How do these factors affect each other?

- What assumptions were made in completing this chart? (Commercial costs less than organic)

- How do all 3 factors affect each other simultaneously?

- What other factors are affected?

Activity 9: Decision Trees

Purpose: To create a framework for planning for the future.
To develop decision-making skills.
To develop teamwork skills.

Roles*   Facilitator, Recorder, Timekeeper, Process Observer

Activity:

a.   Give each group a large piece of newsprint and marker and ask them to choose roles.

b.   Ask each group to choose a question to pursue that relates to their problem, a question that begins with "should."

c.   The question should lead to the first decision point, such as "is it necessary?" Above each decision point, students draw two branches, yes and no, and choose appropriate decisions that arise from these answers. See example in Figure 4:3.

d.   Continue to develop the tree as far as possible to arrive at various futures for this question.

e.   Each group posts their tree for all to observe before a group discussion.

Discussion Questions:
   • What did you learn from this exercise?

   • How did your group work together?

   • What was frustrating about this activity?

   • What else do you need to know to create these futures?

   • How well does a tree represent the future? What other shapes or designs might work?

   • If the original question were worded differently, how different would each tree be?

   • How might your group take action to ensure a positive future rather than a negative one?

*Role definitions are listed on page 122.

Adapted with permission from the National Council for the Social Studies from Fitch & Svengalis (1970) Futures unlimited. Washington DC: NCSS.

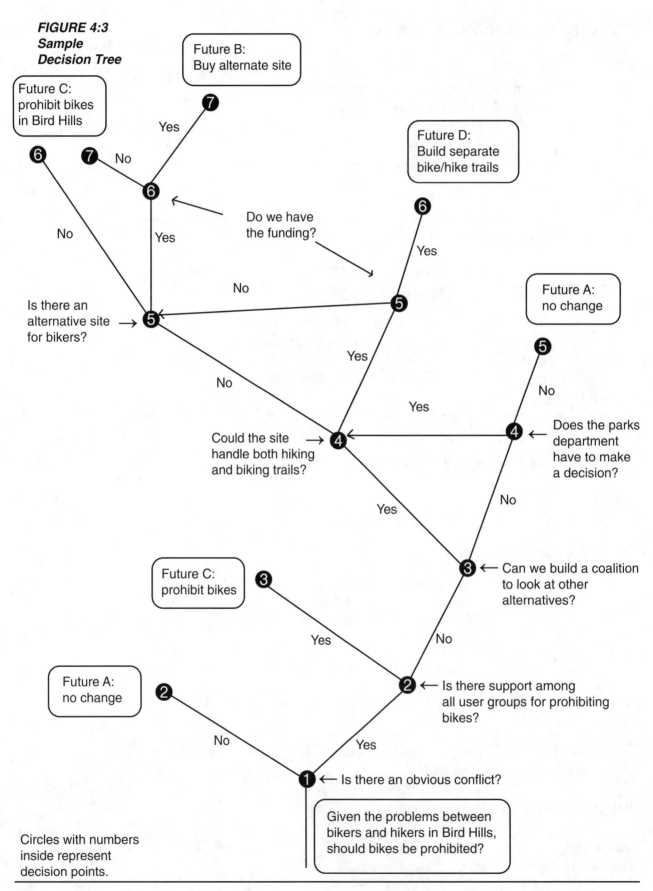

**FIGURE 4:3
Sample
Decision Tree**

Future C:
prohibit bikes
in Bird Hills

Future B:
Buy alternate site

Future D:
Build separate
bike/hike trails

7

Yes

7   No

6

6

No

Yes

Do we have
the funding?

Future A:
no change

6

5

No

Yes

Is there an
alternative site →
for bikers?

5

No

5

Yes

Yes

No

Does the parks
department
have to make
a decision?

Could the site →
handle both hiking
and biking trails?

4   ←

Yes

4

No

Yes

No

Future C:
prohibit bikes

3   ← Can we build a coalition
to look at other
alternatives?

3

Yes

No

Future A:
no change

2   ← Is there support among
all user groups for prohibiting
bikes?

2

No

Yes

1   ← Is there an obvious conflict?

Given the problems between
bikers and hikers in Bird Hills,
should bikes be prohibited?

Circles with numbers
inside represent
decision points.

Activity 10: Futures Wheel

Purpose: To analyze the consequences of an action.
To draw from the knowledge within a group.
To develop teamwork.

Roles: Facilitator, Recorder, Timekeeper, Process Observer

Activity:

a. Distribute one large piece of paper and marker to each group and ask them to choose roles.

b. Ask each group to write a future action in the center of the page.

c. Each group identifies consequences that result from this action and draws them on the page in radiating spokes. See example in Figure 4:4.

d. Second- and third-level consequences are drawn on the wheel radiating from their sources.

e. Each group posts their wheels for all to consider before the group discussion.

Discussion Questions:

• What difficulties did your group face?

• What do you need to know more about to predict the future?

• What consequences surprised you?

• Are there negative and positive reactions from the same future? Why?

• How do the various wheels compare?

• Are there strategies that would ensure a positive future and avoid the negative ones?

• How might this exercise help you create an action plan for a positive future?

*Role definitions are listed on page 122.

Adapted with permission from the National Council for the Social Studies from Fitch & Svengalis (1970) Futures unlimited. Washington DC: NCSS.

FIGURE 4:4
Futures Wheel

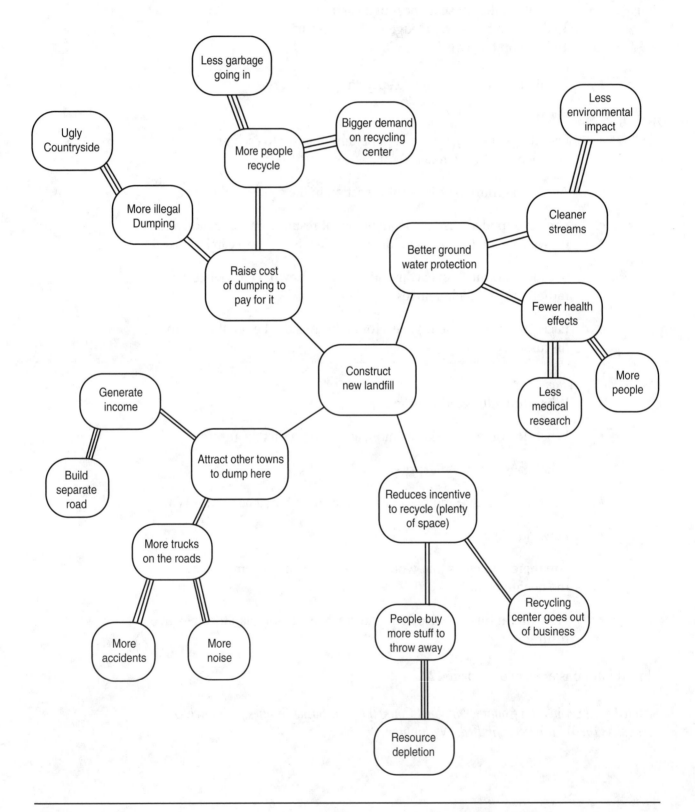

Activity 11: Force Field Analysis

Purpose: To develop abilities to recognize and define problems.
To develop alternatives.
To evaluate alternatives.
To work as a team.
To deepen the understanding of the problem and solutions.

Roles: Facilitator, Recorder, Timekeeper, Process Observer

Activity:

a. Divide the group into smaller groups of 4 or 5 and ask them to choose roles.

b. Distribute a handout to each group.

c. Ask members of each group to decide on a problem and a goal that they wish to pursue for this activity.

d. Ask each group to complete the page, considering the forces that act on the problem the group members have chosen to explore and the resources needed to achieve the goal.

Discussion Questions:

• What are the possible advantages of using this strategy to help think through solutions to problems?

• How was leadership handled in your group?

• What surprised you from this exercise?

• How was your analysis similar to and different from other groups' analysis?

• How well did the group agree on what to write down?

• How might your actions change the analysis you have made about the action you propose?

*Role definitions are listed on page 122.

Reprinted with permission from Stapp, W. B. & Cox, D. A. (1979) Environmental education activities manual. Dexter, MI: Thomson-Shore.

Force Field Analysis Worksheet

The Problem:

The Goal:

Driving Forces:	**Retaining Forces:**

Possible Actions:

Resources we have:

Resources we need:

Activity 12: Environmental Issues Forum

An issues forum, such as might occur with the Environmental Issues Forum (EIF) materials produced by NAAEE, engages learners in a discussion of the advantages and disadvantages of choices in resolving an issue. It may be used to introduce a complex issue or to help learners move through the solution space without focusing on a single answer. In addition, the choices help learners think about the underlying value decisions that accompany each choice.

Purpose: To help learners identify a range of alternatives.
To help learners see multiple perspectives.
To help learners understand that a variety of other opinions are good choices.

Materials: Issue books, moderator guides, and training materials are available from the North American Association for Environmental Education office (PO Box 400, Troy OH 45373, phone: 513–676–2514). Issue books on social issues (National Issues Forum) are produced by the Kettering Foundation (100 Commons Road, Dayton OH 45459–2777, phone: 800–433–7834), and are available from the Kendall/Hunt Publishing Company (2460 Kerper Blvd., Dubuque IO 52004-0539, phone: 800–338–5578).

Activity:

    a.   Encourage participants to review the issue book before the forum.

    b.   During the forum, ask participants to state the advantages and disadvantages of each of the choices.

    c.   Engage participants in questioning and responding to each other, asking if they agree, if they have examples, and what a critic might say of this perspective.

    d.   Make the value implications clear to participants by asking about priorities, why choices are bad, and what difference certain policies might make to the affected parties and the unaffected parties.

    e.   Close the forum by asking participants to sum up the new perspectives they've gained or the common values they've heard expressed.

Step 3: IMPLEMENTING AND EVALUATING ACTIONS

As we have explained, the traditional definition of "problem solving" ends when a solution has been identified. But if the goal is to actually solve the problem, a host of other skills must be tacked on that involve taking action and seeing a solution implemented in the real world. Those skills make up Step 3.

The most obvious classroom activity is action taking itself. There are several resources that help teachers prepare for establishing a class action project, listed below. There are also steps along the way of taking action where skill-building exercises might be useful: arriving at important criteria for decision making, analyzing the value of alternative actions, comparing consequences of various actions, and building a coalition of people and groups who have a stake in the outcome. The following resources can help provide suggestions of ways to tackle these and other skills:

- ***Investigating and Evaluating Environmental Issues and Actions***
  (Hungerford et al., 1985, Stipes Publishing Co, 10-12 Chester St. Champaign IL 61820).
- ***The Action Research and Community Problem Solving Manual***
  (Stapp et al., 1994, c/o GREEN, 721 E. Huron, Ann Arbor MI 48104, 313-761-8142).
- ***The Kid's Guide to Social Action***
  (Lewis, 1991, Minneapolis: Free Spirit)
- ***Training Student Organizers Curriculum***
  (Council on Environment of New York City, 1990, 51 Chambers St., Room 228, New York NY 10007)
- ***E^2: Environment and Education*** *(Formerly the Earth Time Project)*
  (881 Alma Real Drive, Suite 118, Pacific Palisades, CA 90272, 310-573-9608)
- ***Approaching Environmental Issues in the Classroom***
  (NCEET, School of Natural Resources and Environment, University of Michigan, Ann Arbor, MI 48109-1115).

For teachers who may not be able to implement an action plan, there are other ways to help students understand what action taking is about and build confidence in their abilities to embark on such a project. The use of case studies, stories, and examples play a critical role here. The National Consortium for Environmental Education and Training (NCEET) offers some suggestions to teachers of ways to use such materials in the classroom. The Success Story Primer and accompanying collection of environmental success stories are available from NCEET, School of Natural Resources and Environment, University of Michigan, Ann Arbor MI 48109–1115, phone: 313–998–6726.

Analyzing a series of cases helps students think about possibilities and build a framework of action taking. The following activity is one way teachers can introduce an analysis process that can be used throughout the year as more examples are added.

Activity 13: Action Matrix

Purpose: To develop a systematic way to discuss strategies to solve environmental problems.
To share actual examples of actions.
To facilitate future discussions of personal action.

Activity:

a.   With the group, discuss who (in broad terms) is capable of solving environmental problems. Identify 3 to 4 categories (individuals, groups, government, and business are often identified).

b.   Ask who motivates these Problem Solvers to take action. Assist the students in seeing that other people in the same categories are involved (other groups, other government agencies, etc.). Explain that while these entities are the Problem Solvers, they are also the Motivators.

c.   Distribute a matrix with Motivators across the top and Problem Solvers down the side (Handout 2). Ask students to use the cases they have covered and their imagination to fill in the boxes with examples of actions the Motivators use to get the Problem Solvers to take action. See example in Figure 4:5.

d.   In small groups, complete the matrix. Compare examples in all the cells and make one very thorough matrix for the class to use from time to time.

Discussion Questions:

•   What can you as an individual do to help solve problems?

•   If you join a group, what additional activities might you do?

•   How might these individual and group actions influence other actions? Using an example, how might a series of actions be staged to motivate certain behavior on this matrix?

•   As additional examples come before the class, ask the class to identify the cells in the matrix that were used to solve the problem.

•   When are some actions more appropriate than others?

Adapted with permission from Monroe , M. C. (1990) "Converting 'It's no use' into 'Hey, there's a lot I can do:' A matrix for environmental action taking." In Setting the agenda for the 90's. Troy, OH: NAAEE.

A Framework for Analyzing
Environmental Endeavors

MOTIVATORS

PROBLEM SOLVERS	Individuals	Environmental Groups	Government	Business/ Industry
Individuals				
Environmental Groups				
Government				
Business/ Industry				

FIGURE 4:5
Action Matrix
Example

A Framework for Analyzing
Environmental Endeavors

MOTIVATORS

	Individuals	Environmental Groups	Government	Business/ Industry
PROBLEM SOLVERS **Individuals**	Educate yourself Change lifestyle Letters to newspaper Teach and talk to others Participate	Provide information Persuade Advertise Create educational materials	Regulate Tax Provide incentives Provide information Create educational materials	Provide jobs Advertise Make/limit options Create educational materials
Environmental Groups	Join Write letters Give money Elect leaders Become a leader Influence group's agenda	Build coalitions Persuade Inform people Create networks	Research Lobby Regulate Give grants Change tax status	Research Donations Grants Provide jobs Endorsements
Government	Vote Write letters Run for office Raise funds Speak at public hearings	Research Monitor Lobby Bring lawsuits Endorse Speak at public hearings	Make appointments Give grants Charge fees Provide checks/ balances Implement regulations	Provide jobs File lawsuits Lobby Give money Advertise PACs
Business/ Industry	Buy product Boycott product Write letters Buy stock Invest Report violations Draw media attention	Collect data Survey File lawsuit Lead boycott Monitor Create incentives	Create incentives File lawsuit Fine Regulate License Contract Zone	Compete with price and quality File lawsuit Advertise Share technology Cooperate

Role Descriptions for Some Activities

The following roles referred to in this chapter may be helpful for small group activities. Giving each member a function helps share responsibility, develop skills, and reduce management problems.

Facilitator
- Keeps the process moving.
- Ensures that everyone participates.
- Helps group to reach its goal.
- If the group discussion stops, suggests a new way of thinking.

Recorder
- Writes down the actions of the group.
- Acts as the "group memory" by reminding the group of its actions.

Timekeeper
- Keeps the group on time.
- Reminds the group when the time for the activity is almost gone.

Process Observer
- Observes the work of the group, making a few notes.
- Reports back on the process at the end of the activity.

Prober
- Asks questions to help people explain how they see the world differently.
- Gives examples or situations to which people respond.

APPENDIX:
FULL TEXT OF PRACTITIONER DESCRIPTIONS

Teach About Geese
JANET CARRIER ADY, U.S. FISH AND WILDLIFE SERVICE, WASHINGTON, D.C.

Populations of four species of geese that nest in Alaska's Yukon-Kuskokwim Delta and migrate and winter along the Pacific Flyway have declined severely. The Yukon-Kuskokwim Delta Goose Management Plan provides a cooperative framework for research and management efforts dedicated to reversing the goose population decline. Traditionally, Native Alaskans harvested geese and their eggs to supplement a subsistence lifestyle. As compliance with the plan initially was voluntary on the part of the people of the Y-K Delta, one vital aspect was the establishment of an Alaskan information and education task force. The task force created a myriad of products and programs to inform Pacific Flyway residents about the plan. A calendar poster contest, comic book, and visits to the schools by resident Native Alaskans working for the U.S. Fish and Wildlife Service made students aware of important concepts relating to the goose issue. The "Teach About Geese" curriculum was developed as a more comprehensive curriculum for use during the school year.

The Teach About Geese materials include adaptations of existing materials and development of new activities designed to address local needs and concerns. Input from the ultimate users, teachers and students, was solicited through a series of field testing workshops, and original activities were developed with their assistance. A cooperative effort among many individuals and agencies provided training and credit courses for rural Alaska teachers, and ownership and credibility among environmental educators statewide.

The Teach About Geese curriculum represents more than informational materials. It represents an extension of scientific research to the public through education and teaching about critical wildlife issues through experiential learning. Excellent available materials were adapted to meet local needs and concerns. An issue concerning a resource shared by people along the Pacific Flyway is being addressed with a voluntary, educational approach. Teach About Geese meets needs of kids for relevant study topics, of teachers for localized materials, and of agencies for long-term solutions to a resource/human problem.

Harvest of the four species of geese declined in the late 1980s, subsequent to the Information and Education program, of which Teach About Geese was an integral part. The exact amount of the decreased harvest and increased populations attributable specifically to the Teach About Geese portion of the overall Information and

Education Program is difficult to ascertain. However, an evaluation conducted by Dave Case in 1989 revealed strong support for the school education program. Teachers and principals were receptive to the education program and were using it with their classes. Students were learning about geese, migration, wetlands, and related ecological concepts. Students were sharing information about geese with their parents, and behavior toward geese changed as a result.

Villagers and teachers provided suggestions regarding improvements to the program, which were included in the Case report. Most of these recommendations had been implemented by 1993, however a second evaluation has not been conducted. Workshops for teachers have continued, and feedback is requested from all who receive the materials. These comments are incorporated into the program when possible. A school art contest for a calendar continues to be popular. A family who had a winner in the contest decided it would not be right to catch goslings and collect eggs from one of the four goose species, since their child had won the contest. That was significant, as Case reports, not only because the family did not take the geese, but also because it was comfortably reported to peers in a high school classroom, indicating cultural acceptance of the plan.

The school program was but one element of a comprehensive information and education program designed to target a specific wildlife issue. The management problem and the context of the management situation were investigated before educational and management strategies were developed. The special interests of the people who had the closest contacts with the geese were identified with research about the people and their culture. A multifaceted approach using a variety of educational activities and methods was adopted. Local involvement and responsibility, including participation of native leaders and residents in both the management plans and education and communication programs, contribute greatly to the program's success. The reduction in harvest of geese was influenced greatly by the fact that opinions of local residents were incorporated into the management process by agency decision makers.

The educational strategies also involved cooperative planning and shared responsibilities by teachers, environmental educators, and community members. The activities used with teachers and students were experiential and "hands-on." The materials were developed with local input by teachers who dealt with the students daily. The teacher workshops and village meetings included face-to-face contact with Fish and Wildlife Service managers so that the questions about the geese could be addressed. A particularly important group of service employees was the Refuge Information Technicians (RIT's), local, Yupik-speaking residents who traveled to village meetings and were often a part of the teacher workshops. The quality and completeness of the curriculum materials made teacher implementation as easy as possible. The variety of materials, such as posters, videos, art materials, and even a board game, provided something for every learning style. Although not extensive, the evaluation component of the program helped fine-tune and improve weaker areas and recognize program strengths.

Care for Wetland Birds
JANIS ALBRIGHT-BURTON, MANOMET BIRD OBSERVATORY, MASSACHUSETTS

Middleborough, Massachusetts, is a small community in New England that, like many other towns, is faced with rapid development that threatens both surface and ground waters. To protect its future water supply, the town acquired the Pratt Farm and its fragile wetlands. Recognizing that mere ownership may not protect the water supply, the Conservation Commission asked Manomet Bird Observatory to develop a program that would help Middleborough residents develop the skills needed to plan for and protect the wetland.

Manomet Bird Observatory (MBO) is a nonprofit environmental research and education center 50 miles south of Boston. During planning sessions in 1990, we met with parents, teachers, and community leaders before targeting "Care for Wetland Birds" for fifth-grade classes. The upper elementary grades had expressed an interest in using Pratt Farm as an outdoor teaching center for local ecosystems, a part of their curriculum. During 1991, Manomet worked side by side with the community to train teachers, students, and parents about wetland ecology and the tools needed to deal with local water issues. Our format consisted of workshops, classroom and field sessions, creation of a teacher and parent resource guide, and ongoing evaluation. Specific program content included an introduction to types of wetlands, understanding the value of wetlands on a local and global scale, and using birds as environmental monitors based on MBO heron and shorebird studies. Problem solving skills included (1) defining local wetland issues; (2) becoming informed through field sessions, art activities, and readings; (3) identifying and choosing solutions; and (4) developing individual plans of action. Finally, classes learned research techniques such as using binoculars, keeping a nature journal, and conducting simple pollution experiments.

Our program differed from the typical science program in two ways. First, teachers wanted a strong art component to help students strengthen their observation skills and to meet the needs of different learning styles. Second, the program allowed teachers to incorporate local issues into their Texas-based science texts. For example, students studied the decline of specific wetland birds in Massachusetts that corre-lated with habitat degradation based on MBO's long-term banding data.

To monitor the success of "Care for Wetland Birds," we incorporated a formative evaluation, in the form of student questionnaires and informal teacher interviews throughout the project. We also followed with a summative evaluation question-naire. Our evaluation findings lead us to believe that the model worked. First, teachers commented that students seemed ready to "handle" a field trip after the program's art experience of sketching natural details in the schoolyard and keeping a journal. By the time Pratt Farm field sessions occurred, classes were ready to use their field experience to develop critical thinking skills. For example, they quickly identified local problems with their streams and began to brainstorm their own solutions to these challenges.

Second, our qualitative evaluation showed the great value of a research-school partnership. Before the project, only 9% of the students cited reasons other than wildlife for protecting wetlands. After the program, 46% offered other values of the wetland ecosystem. The close access to MBO's scientific staff helped broaden the students' perceptions.

In addition, other factors were important to the program's success. According to a recent National Science Board Study, many elementary teachers lack the science background needed to teach effectively and accurately. It is presumptive to assume that all teachers know and completely understand complex concepts such as environmental monitoring or watersheds. Yet how can we begin to ask teachers to help their students propose solutions if the teachers themselves lack this background? Again, through our strong scientific partnership, we provided teachers with a solid foundation during the workshops. With this knowledge, they then had the confidence to help students analyze local wetland issues and propose solutions.

Because the program genuinely met a town need, it had active community support. Town volunteers participated in the teacher workshops and in turn helped teach during the field sessions rather than assuming the traditional chaperon role. In addition, parents wanted to instill in their children the importance of the project. The Pratt Farm Committee publicized the program in papers and held art contests. The library developed a list of important wetland reference books to buy for children and adults. This momentum was very exciting and the children responded enthusiastically. As a result, the students took the issue very seriously.

In summary, we would recommend the following based on our experience: First, be sure that your teacher training includes a strong science foundation, and use local scientists as part of your community resources. Second, and this especially applies to projects with limited time and budgets, help students develop problem solving solutions that speak to their own interests and are "doable." For example, some fifth graders proposed putting up bird houses to increase wildlife diversity, while others wrote letters against the airport that was proposed near their wetlands. Small steps and personal ideas are a good starting point for participants who are just beginning to develop problem solving skills. Finally, build a solid community foundation so that when you step back at the end, you really are not needed anymore! This paradox is the final proof of a program's success.

Using Technology in Problem Solving
IVAN BAUGH, COMPUTER RESOURCE TEACHER, KENTUCKY

Students, when informed about environmental problems and how those problems affect their world of tomorrow, want change. Technology empowers students to grasp the seriousness of the problems, to understand their personal relationship to problems, and to make changes that help solve the problems. Teachers, working under a U.S. Department of Education grant, developed a technology-centered environmental science curriculum incorporating word processing, database, spreadsheet, telecommunications, electronic research, HyperCard, and interactive multimedia activities. Those tools help students as they encounter a problem, investigate it to determine environmental impact, identify contributors, enumerate the consequences of unchanged behaviors, propose achievable solutions that reflect sound scientific reasoning, and communicate their findings.

Curriculum topics include Principles of Ecology, Environmental Management, Soil and Water Management, Water and Air Pollution, and Energy and the Environment. Students examine environmental causes and effects for the identified problems using the previously listed resources. In one case, they create spreadsheets that measure the quantity of hot water used for personal hygiene, calculate the amount of energy needed to heat the water, enumerate related environmental problems generated by energy consumption and water disposal, investigate methods of reducing water consumption and energy use, and project the outcomes of these proposed changes. They use graphs to illustrate the level of significance of their findings and the benefits of their projected changes. The students then write reports, using integrated applications software to communicate their findings, and propose and promote solutions.

In another project, students compared the quantity of garbage generated in the community with the space needed to accommodate it in a landfill. Interactive multimedia defined the immensity of the problem and the environmental pollutants associated with transporting and storing the garbage. The numbers gained relevance as the students used a spreadsheet to determine the number of classrooms one day's garbage would fill. They looked at the cyclic nature of various disposal methods and studied the byproducts of the decaying garbage and incineration. A HyperCard simulation showed the benefits of recycling, as students function as sanitation engineers sorting the garbage into recycling bins. The impact of these activities increases significantly when the data shows the entire class how much of a difference they can each make. Recycling bins in the classroom and/or the school gave students a chance to influence their peers.

This program sees the student as knowledge-worker. The teacher is a facilitator of learning, not a dispenser of knowledge, and participates as a member of the learning team. Active learning provides ownership, demonstrating how each individual counts. By working with personal data (e.g., water usage, garbage generation, automobile use habits, energy use, and recycling) students become more committed to change. The program incorporates the scientific method while reducing the "I can't make any difference" syndrome. We revisit topics periodically during the year to gather evidence of behavior changes while reinforcing the concepts. The students practice leadership in developing and executing school-based campaigns; here they apply what they know for a real audience, not just the teacher's eyes. School newspapers have become a vehicle for sharing the findings and promoting change.

Teachers report students show surprise at the impact of their personal behaviors on the environment. Students promote change because they realize their world will be less livable if they do not. Individuals personally adopt specific behaviors as a natural outgrowth of the study. Student leadership in the home, likewise, encourages family changes and extends the sphere of influence for the individual. Some classes organize school-wide projects for the community. Students gain marketable skills that prepare them for the work world.

Changes occur because the students' investigations relate directly to personal behaviors and problems with which they identify. Scientific understanding increases because the content relates to life. Technology facilitates accumulation and interpretation of the data, reducing the tedium and eliminating computation problems for students with limited statistical skills. They develop functional skills and useful pre-work experience. Some personal data provides information about the sources of environmental problems; changes in personal behavior occur as the individuals realize the degree of difference they make. The learners complete activities that accommodate varied learning styles and provide authentic assessments. They realize personal behaviors contribute to problems they would like to avoid. Their interaction with peers, family, faculty, and community produces changes.

Three key elements of this program include
1. using technology to accumulate, assimilate, and integrate the gathered data;

2. authentic performances for measuring comprehension of identified problems and adoption of change; and

3. recognized connections to daily living. Students using technology to address the studied concepts showed academic improvement over those taught traditionally.

Learning to Solve Complex Environmental Issues
Aɴɴᴇ Cᴀᴍᴏᴢᴢɪ, EᴄᴏLᴏɢɪᴄ, Aɴᴛɪɢᴏɴɪsʜ, Nᴏᴠᴀ Sᴄᴏᴛɪᴀ

I bet you we could come up with an idea to figure out how to stop the holes from forming in the ozone layer. I bet you there's an easy solution that nobody has figured out because it's too easy. Maybe we make things more complicated because we don't really examine the problem.

This realization emerged from a 13-year-old boy's participation in a problem solving communications game I adapted from Adult Human Resource Development Training. Many of the games and activities designed for adults are easily applicable for use with younger people and are particularly important when dealing with environmental issues. The interactive, participatory, and problem solving components of such practices should not be ignored when designing problem solving activities for youth.

This particular activity, Hollow Squares (Pfeiffer & Jones, 1974) asks groups of students to form five squares of equal size with the pieces they are given. The squares use pieces of different sizes and shapes. Each team consists of planners, implementers, and observers. By giving several pieces of different squares to each person, and challenging them not to speak during the process, the game can be adapted to different ages and abilities.

I use this game to teach problem solving skills because

1. it is challenging, fun, and relatively easy to facilitate;

2. its use of the team approach provides students with a different and often new perspective that allows them to view their teammates in a different way;

3. it illustrates the complexity of problems and the cooperative, creative thinking required to solve them.

Students are responsible for the outcome of the game; the teacher is simply the facilitator or guide, who explains and distributes the rules. I have often used two teams at once and added the additional component of a competition between the two teams. Competition works particularly well with eighth graders, but I have had success with senior high students and even younger children.

To solve the puzzle, the team must communicate effectively, listen well to instructions, and think creatively. The solution to the puzzle isn't an obvious choice, but it is an easy one. After the exercise is finished, the facilitator asks the observers to discuss the problem solving processes used and to examine the weaknesses and strengths of the group.

At this point, I introduce a local environmental issue and ask the students to brainstorm in their groups about solutions to the problem using the skills they have learned by playing Hollow Squares. Although it is best to have the discussion of the game and environmental issue immediately, given the school setting, this can take place in the next class. The follow-up discussion is critical; the facilitator should carefully structure and develop it. The total playing time is about 1 hour. The success of the team depends largely on how well the team members have listened to the facilitator, how well they have read their instructions, and whether or not they impose extra rules. The students often talk about how they imposed rules on themselves that were unnecessary.

Students often are frustrated with the activity, particularly if they do not find an easy solution. This frustration inevitably enhances their learning and should not be considered a "negative." Nevertheless, students are energetic and excited as they play the game, and show an obvious understanding of the relationship of the game to environmental problem solving. Students find the game really makes them think and, invariably, they enjoy it!

Student comments have convinced me that the game effectively develops problem solving skills. Students learn the value of cooperation, even when it is difficult. The team observers often point out that when one individual tries to solve the problem alone, the group fails. On the other hand, when a group is successful, the student observers typically point out how well everyone worked together.

Everyone has a clear role. The decision about how to play that role requires a level of thinking about "self." The constructive feedback provided to each student in the discussion helps students analyze their own strengths and weaknesses. Finally, the game encourages new roles and problem solving behaviors for students to try out in a safe, fun environment. One of my students wrote:

> *When we first started playing I didn't think I would be able to do anything because I'm quiet and shy and nobody listens to my ideas. When I came up with the idea, my group actually listened and then we won! It gave me more confidence to express my ideas. I think we can use this to solve problems. Maybe there are a lot of people out there who have good ideas about how to solve something but they don't know how to say it. I liked working in a team because when we put our ideas together it was easier to solve and I don't think I would have said my idea out loud in a big group if you had asked us. It was fun, too!*

Reference

Pfeiffer, J.W. & Jones, J.E. (1974). *The handbook of structured experiences for human relations training* (Vol.1). San Diego, CA: University Associates.

Project NatureConnect:
MICHAEL J. COHEN, WORLD PEACE UNIVERSITY, WASHINGTON

On an average, we spend over 95% of our lives indoors. Even when we are out-doors, we think predominantly in languaged, cultural ways that are foreign to Nature's workings. Predictably, our extreme separation from the natural world creates problems. Because we are not bonded to the natural environment, we don't feel it and are not motivated to act on its behalf. It makes sense for modern people to learn to find, trust, and integrate Nature's time-tested problem solving processes.

A powerful new learning process, Project NatureConnect, motivates affirmative action in people who are uncomfortable with, or suffer from, our culture's destruc-tive ways. Project NatureConnect experientially, scientifically, and cross culturally lets Nature teach its wisdom. Its unique interdisciplinary activities take place in natural settings: wilderness, backyards, terrariums, or person to person—anywhere people can sense Nature's attractions.

The project offers a self-empowering field guide to activities that make it possible to connect and bond with nature any time, any place. The activities create teachable moments in which the natural world resonates in us. The ensuing thoughts, feelings, and reactions trigger more discussion, sharing, and analysis.

The activities ask learners to think critically and to articulate their natural connections, what they sense and feel while in a natural area or while in contact with the inner nature of another person. Some activities require learners to spend time in a natural area with others engaged in the following pursuits:

Learning how to make their mind "blank" in order to sense, without words or reasoning, the attractions they discover in a natural place and/or in a person's inner nature (inner child)—attractions such as colors, moods, motions, feelings, textures, fragrances, designs, beauty, and so forth.

Labeling what they experience as *connections* rather than as objects. For example, an attraction to the color, motion, or sound of a person, waterfall, or a bird is termed a *natural connection* or *natural attraction* rather than a *person, place, or thing*.

Validating that each natural connection feels good; a natural nonlanguage experience is enjoyable and nurturing; the existence of their attraction to a natural object is as natural and factual as the object itself; writing about, reading about, or discussing these attractions feels comfortable and creates interpersonal connections.

From 30 years of personal outdoor research, Project NatureConnect teaches learners to trust their unmediated experiences in nature. For example, we biologically inherit not 5, but over 53 natural senses which pervade the natural world. We experience senses of hunger, thirst, compassion, place, language, gravity, form, and motion. These natural sensations and feelings are "inventions" of Nature, not culture. Nature seldom works with words and beliefs. Sensitivity to natural senses is how Nature intelligently solves problems, grows, and survives.

While our cultural upbringing believes in strengthening our senses of sight, reason, and language, it often neglects or demeans our 50 other natural senses as immaterial, subjective irrationality. Problems result, for our withdrawn natural senses are essential building blocks for environmental bonding, peace, self-esteem, and stress management. Project NatureConnect works because it reverses this process. It entices and rewards our honed senses of reasoning and language to seek, awaken, enjoy, validate, resonate with, trust, and appreciate our many other natural senses. The process regenerates roots that ground us to Earth. It reduces the stress that causes apathy and dysfunction. It catalyzes bonds to the natural world which create environmental and socially responsible relationships.

The project's three keys to success are that it

a. catalyzes and validates unmediated contact with the natural world;

b. awakens and scientifically identifies over 53 sensations and feelings as unmediated attractions and callings of the natural world; and

c. evokes sharing, reasoning, and discussion that translate sensory experiences in natural areas into motivated, unifying, environmentally and socially responsible acts.

Swarthmore College Environmental Education

PETER BLAZE CORCORAN, BATES COLLEGE, MAINE
ERIC SIEVERS, 1992 SWARTHMORE COLLEGE GRADUATE

> *I know I love this Earth, and that's taking me places, and giving me certainty.*
> *So what does Emilio do with this love? Well, first of all, I teach. I teach in*
> *the way that I want to, with emotion, and energy, and passion, and honesty,*
> *and full of humor and love.* —Emilio Spadola, EE student, Fall 1991

Emilio and his peers energized the environmental studies program at Swarthmore College through their passionate and reflective participation in our course, Environmental Education (EE). It had four goals: to achieve a broad perspective of the field of contemporary environmental education—its theory, practice, research, and relationship to other fields; to develop an historical and a futures perspective of the field—its roots in nature study and science education and its prospects for the future; to broaden and enrich the personal experience of nature; and to extend individual teaching skills in environmental education. The course's aim was to discover the philosophical and methodological power of environmental education to solve problems, both environmental and educational.

We gathered twice a week for 75 minutes (often longer) and almost always outside, more than once in the rain. The curriculum included diverse reading assignments. Some attended to the ecological crisis and to the history and theory of EE (Rachel Carson, Aldo Leopold, Harold Hungerford, Bill Stapp, Noel McInnis, Joseph Cornell, Bill McKibben, Joanna Macy, Noel Gough, Charlene Spretnak, Thomas Berry, Giovanna DiChiro, and John Huckle to name a few). Others examined different sociopolitical critiques of the ecological crisis and the possible applications to EE (ecofeminism, deep ecology, bioregionalism). Class time was devoted almost fully to discussion and student presentations, student teaching projects, and student-led opening activities. Some of the projects and assignments included teaching with local museums or at-risk after-school programs, development of a curriculum mini-unit, attendance at a professional conference, participation in a Council of All Beings with John Seed, workshops on urban EE with Mike Weilbacher, and Native American storytelling with Michael Caduto. Appreciable time was given to considering a diversity of perspectives on nature as chosen and presented by the students, ranging from that of an Oregon lumberjack to a young urban child, from a wood-gathering Third World woman to a human virus.

The course was intended to be a model of effective environmental education, not simply an explanation of it. Accordingly, in many respects, this course distinguished itself pedagogically from traditional college instruction. The course represented an opportunity to incorporate ethics and philosophy into a program of environmental studies. The classroom was nonhierarchical. Discussions replaced lectures, participation in class activities emphasized cooperation over competition, and interdisciplinary approaches to problem solving were pursued. The development of a close community in the classroom encouraged emotional expression as well as intellectual exploration, allowing students to express despair over the ecological crisis as well as hope for the resolution of environmental problems.

From the beginning, a positive attitude and high energy level characterized the course. Students were amazed it existed, celebrated its potential, and expressed gratitude in the form of dynamic participation. This course directly addressed students' lives, their interests, and their experiences; it had relevance to students teaching at summer camps, members of Earthlust! (the student environmental activist organization), preservice teachers, and anyone concerned with the ecological crisis. It encouraged students to evaluate their own educational experiences, and allowed them to share and compare those thoughts with others in the group. As a result, a dialogue about educational philosophy and its problem solving capability was engendered. Most important, this course validated student concern with the ecological crisis and facilitated their drawing upon friends, inspired individuals, and community introspection to put that concern into perspective.

It is bold to say that one course changed people's lives, but student letters, evaluations, and comments credit the course with influencing decisions about pursuing environmental education professionally, changing majors, facilitating better communication, challenging the Swarthmore curriculum, and appreciating nature. Several students are continuing teaching projects, many are eyeing EE positions, a few are writing children's books, and some are working with faculty to develop environmental courses and course components. Students appreciate the opportunity to explore different philosophical approaches to the ecological crisis and the educational process, and posit that breadth of viewpoint is an invaluable resource in fostering confidence in personal and political problem solving.

Daniel Wright, a sophomore who dropped his engineering major, comments, "I have decided to go into education because....I love the curiosity in children, and I would love to see a future generation which openly questions the wisdom of each and every social practice. 'Why, why, why?' is what children say when they are young, but then they transform into acceptors of 'the facts' that are the backbone of education....Through my EE class, my awareness in both environmental and educational issues has grown and transformed me."

It is difficult to assess the quantitative impact of this course on students' problem solving processes. Indeed, the diversity of responses and future plans reported by the students testifies to a wide range of thought. Some, like Daniel, have professed their desire to enter education; others look forward to creative careers in the natural sciences and engineering. It would be unfair to claim that this course alone taught students to think critically or to validate ethics and emotion in problem-solving processes. Yet, we know it strengthened skills and enhanced students' abilities to apply them to environmental and educational problems.

In our view, three factors contributed to the course's capacity to help students solve problems. First, the content of the course was relevant to their lives, interests, and experiences. Second, the course accommodated their creativity and critical suggestions. Third, it provided the support of a close community. Taken together, this relevance, creativity, and support generated a hopeful and impassioned approach to environmental and educational problem solving.

Urban Teacher Education in Environmental Science:
Let's Start with the Issues

CAROL FIALKOWSKI, CHICAGO ACADEMY OF SCIENCES, ILLINOIS

The Environmental Issues Forum (EIF) is a series of four graduate courses for urban K-8 teachers. Each course carries 1 hour of science education credit through National Louis University. The courses are offered at the Chicago Academy of Sciences, located in the heart of the city. Generally, one course is offered each session, so over a year, teachers can complete the cycle and receive a total of four credits. Since fall 1989, approximately 180 teachers have participated in these courses.

Courses are scheduled over a weekend, usually a 6-hour evening or day, followed by a 9-hour day. This design facilitates a morning field trip to a site that illustrates the problem being studied as well as potential solutions. The four courses use the following field trip sites:

1. A coal burning utility plant to study air quality issues.

2. A water reclamation facility to explore water quality issues at the old sewage treatment plant.

3. A landfill with methane reclamation to understand solid waste and recycling.

4. A restored prairie to discuss land use issues.

Each course is designed to mesh methods with content knowledge and each follows this sequence of investigation:

1. What are the issues and problems locally and globally related to the topic?

2. What knowledge and content is necessary to help the learner understand and unravel these problems?

3. Based on this knowledge, what solutions and actions can we, as individuals or as a group of individuals, take to help solve the problem in some way?

The focus of these courses, on problems and their solutions, rather than simply content knowledge, is a new approach for most urban teachers. Illinois has recently mandated four goals for science education in the state and Goal 2 addresses the Science-Technology-Society connection. While fulfilling the directives of this goal, the courses are natural for cross-disciplinary and cooperative group learning. This becomes a very attractive package for teachers wanting to incorporate these new approaches in their teaching. Additionally, the museum offers an outreach program for K-8 students that parallels the content, format, and methods of EIF. The program is entitled Ecological Citizenship (Eco-Cit). Teachers in either the classroom program (Eco-Cit) or the graduate courses (EIF) have priority for participation in the other. This "one-two" punch provides the urban teachers with the continued support needed for implementation of an environmental program so new to most urban areas. Both EIF and Eco-Cit have been supported by the Illinois State Department of Education through grant monies from the state's science literacy initiative.

These quotes from teacher participants attest to the viability of the courses:

- "Informative, educational, increased my knowledge, Wayside Prairie was great!"

- "Students see participatory nature and practical application of material for the classroom. Very student-centered. Can be integrated into other subject areas as well."

- "Hands-on approach to the topic of acid rain, greenhouse effect, ozone. Uses a variety of teaching techniques."

The transfer of course content, approach, and techniques to the teachers is measured by the quality of the curricular units shared and turned in at the reconvene session. Eight weeks after the course ends, all participants return to share ways in which they've successfully used the problem solving approach and activities in their classrooms. Written unit outlines of these lessons are distributed so teachers leave with many new ideas. The enthusiasm, quality, and student response to the teachers' efforts testify to the approach. Videos, photographs, songs, artwork, letters, science fair projects, recycling and clean air campaigns, and water conservation steps have been shared.

The courses in EIF work because they "model the model." In other words, the same approach is used in the courses that the teachers will use in their classrooms—exploring issues and problems, then gaining knowledge and content, and understanding solutions and actions. The courses do not lecture or theorize on how you might teach environmental problem solving—we do it! The teachers learn the same hands-on way they should teach the students. As we observed, compared, contrasted, experimented, analyzed, and synthesized as steps in problem solving, the teachers realize that these same techniques could be transferred to the classroom. The investment and hands-on experience in the process leads to the feeling, "Hey, I can do this!" This form of empowerment is a powerful force.

In summary, the key reasons for EIF's success are:

1. The courses provide teachers with the opportunity for joint problem solving and sharing with peers.

2. The teachers feel empowered to transfer course methods and approaches to their classrooms.

3. The model of issues and problems to knowledge and content to solution and action is adaptable, practical, and relevant in an urban setting.

State and national mandates for curricula that involve problem solving as an essential component are becoming the norm. Environmental issues and concerns are becoming central to the agenda and thinking of the country. Uniting the two in environmental problem solving curricula is a step that addresses and fulfills both concerns—a strong step to "solving both problems."

Solving Environmental Problems Using Learning Styles
Ruth Jacquot, Murray State University, Kentucky

The baggage we bring to a proble solving arena is loaded with preconceptions of arguments, past failures, our own passions, our own prejudices, our indignation, and much more. Some of the baggage brought to the table can be used to aid in problem solving. Knowledge of our own learning style and the style of the other participants in the process is such an aid and has a strong, synergistic effect on the process of problem solving. Learners who know themselves and how they work best, who can find out how the participants in the process prefer to work and how they are most successful can focus on that successful process and aim at reaching consensus.

If environmental problem solvers define themselves as learners and the problem solving process as a learning process, it is not difficult to introduce the concept of learning styles as a problem solving strategy. David Kolb's experiential learning research and theory have been extended by him and others to accomplish this. We all have developed our unique process of experiential learning, which works best for us when we can choose our approach and technique for learning. For example, many people approach the problem of assembling a new "toy" by taking all the parts out of the box, handling them, visualizing the way they fit together, experimenting with them, and then, perhaps, looking for the instruction manual. Others choose to study the manual before unloading the contents, and still others may systematically follow instructions and assemble the item without ever imagining the result. Having the luxury to make the choice is a critical element in this hypothetical case.

Many environmental problems are like this assembly job. The problem may already be defined or it may need to be reframed, but some people will begin by brainstorming a menu of solutions, and some will need to put the statement of the problem into a more usable form or to analyze the actual impact of the problem as they perceive it. Imagine that two assemblers of the reality of the situation have two different styles of learning about it. One wants to handle the parts, see where they fit, and then step back and see what the results of this type of assembly are: a trial and error learner. The other wants to thoroughly analyze the implications of the problem as defined, perhaps reframe the problem, then begin to find a menu of possible solutions. If the leader of a process is intent on imposing a step-by-step approach that cancels the mystery and fun for the intuitive person, the resulting solution can lack creativity, and more importantly lack support from all players.

What is the likelihood of finding common ground in this situation? Very good if learners can approach their differences as a learning style difference and they realize that no style is either right or wrong and then are encouraged to discuss their choice of techniques in light of their own style. This requires self-knowledge, which can be achieved by a short discussion of themselves as voluntary learners and by taking a learning style inventory and being given guidance in the use of the knowledge. If these individuals are going to be working together frequently, it is beneficial to take the time to identify these styles so that the participants are using similar vocabulary and reference points. After taking the inventory and recognizing the learning style differences represented in the group, a thorough discussion of experiential learning theory helps students see an application of their new self-knowledge and knowledge of other's needs. In addition, Kolb's research and writing provide a problem solving model that is empowering and synergistic. It is important to emphasize that this program does not focus on an individual's ability or achievement, only on his or her unique learning style.

This approach recognizes individual differences without judgment, seeks inputs from all by including everyone's choice of technique, and, if done with flexibility, adequate time, and commitment, can bring about a solution that represents the best that the participants have to offer. We can develop empathy for different points of view and different processes of problem solving and learning by approaching them without judgment and with respect for individual differences. To make use of the strengths of individual differences in learning styles, it is imperative that the leader recognize the impact his or her style has on the group process.

In environmental simulations, groups who have been made aware of this process are much more able to separate the process from the value expressed by their classmates. In community meetings where the leader is cognizant of the needs of participants to process information and seek solutions in extremely different ways, opportunities are presented for this difference to operate successfully. For example, the rhythm of a public meeting has been orchestrated to allow for the analytical, reflective learner to study the problem and also for the brainstorming, intuitive concrete learner to explore possible solutions. In arranging problem solving dyads, two learners can use their differences to promote synergistic processes, or, by lack of acceptance of differences in style, come to an early impasse. The difference in outcomes is in the knowledge of individual learning styles and an awareness of the potential of accepting and building on each other's strengths. Research has shown that employees appreciate their supervisor more when their problem-analysis styles are similar, but it is just as likely that these people would appreciate the differences if the differences were pointed out nonjudgmentally and with goodwill.

An important element of problem solving is conflict management. If participants are given the skills to recognize the processes in force, they can make use of these processes—building on strengths rather than focusing on divergent values. Therefore, conflict management can focus on issues, not on differences in approach. In fact, the differences in styles are necessary to focus our strengths and to develop a win/win solution.

The most critical aspects of using differences in styles to achieve understanding is acceptance of these differences as strengths. A leader who is cognizant of the effect of this type of approach and flexible in using it is a key to this positive process. Time is an essential element, but in seeking long-term solutions to work-threatening problems, we need to take the time to achieve lasting solutions.

Reference

Kolb, D.A. Problem management: Learning from experience. In Srivstva, S. (1984). *The executive mind*. Jossey-Bass: San Francisco.

Experiential Environmental Education
DAN KOWAL, EE SPECIALIST AT THE LOGAN SCHOOL, COLORADO

The Logan School for Creative Learning is a private school for gifted and talented children ages 5 to 15. One of the unique features to its alternative class offerings is the environmental education (EE) program. The EE specialist develops an interdisciplinary environmental study with individual teachers and designs specialized field trips that augment the children's learning experience.

The EE program takes on a multifaceted approach toward the development of problem solving skills. All students engage in EE activities. The program is very experiential in nature and provides concrete learning opportunities. Field studies can last for a day to two weeks. Curricular studies last anywhere from a few days to a whole year. By bringing students to the source of what they are studying, the Logan School inspires the students' interest in environmental affairs and offers growth opportunities in the areas of observation, interpretation, analysis, synthesis, and evaluation—skill areas that are crucial to problem solving.

Our students explore the environment (whether it is a city study or a trip to the Oregon coastline) at a pace that allows time for discovery, an affective connection to place, and the contemplation of issues facing an area and its inhabitants. Although students may engage in active research inquiries such as solid waste and ocean pollution, the EE program addresses as many sides of an issue as possible. The goal is to show how conflicts are intricate webs, like ecology, and that several angles must be considered if problems are to be solved. The school may support student solutions to issues, but encourages students to take ownership and direction in these matters so that they can feel a sense of power in making change in the world.

Field studies, role-playing simulations, student involvement in environmental monitoring and/or improvement projects, and outside speakers illustrating problems and problem solving techniques are additional activities to the students' regular agenda at school. In particular, the EE program finds it productive to link students with people who are working toward solving an environmental problem. Students listen to and question speakers who offer them models in dealing with environmental issues. One of the strong points of this presentation is that students can see the dedication and hard work behind a particular project as well as understand the real time factor that goes along with problem solving: change does not happen overnight.

The effectiveness of the EE program is demonstrated by the students' interaction with their teachers and peers. Two years ago, an initial unit on energy conservation and recycling inspired a recycling program that has expanded today. Students analyzed the recycling potential of their classroom, projected energy savings if everyone in the school participated, and convinced the school to establish a program. The feedback from parents also demonstrates how students influence behaviors at home from recycling to energy use. It is not uncommon to hear, "Thanks a lot! My child yelled at me for throwing away a pop can yesterday!"

Students who have been at the school for several years often recall and apply concepts or experiences from earlier curricular/field studies. For example, one student studied plant growth on mine tailings. Although she decided to do this on her own, she mentioned the scientific studies she performed at another mine site the prior year while she brainstormed this project idea.

The concluding sessions of curricular/field studies demonstrate the impact of the EE program's experiential aspect. As stated earlier, the program strives to broaden the students' thinking toward issues. During "wrap-up" times, students often say that they never considered particular viewpoints until they came on a field trip. Some mention that they never understood the complexity of an issue until they were confronted with it face to face. Students comment favorably on having a strong element of control in all activities. As opposed to just reading about an environmental problem in a book or being lectured to, students enjoy examining the situation firsthand and having the latitude to solve things on their own.

Students work in groups in most problem solving activities. Group dynamic skills are crucial to the success of most projects. Therefore, the EE program emphasizes group building and leadership exercises to strengthen the group process skills of each individual. Some field trips are dedicated solely to developing these skills. Throughout many field studies, facilitators relate individual and group initiatives to solving problems in the participants' lives. Another idea behind these programs is to translate the leadership and cooperative behaviors gained in these experiences to problem solving behaviors needed in environmental issues. Many times, these problems seem quite overwhelming. Therefore, the EE program works on building the individual's self-confidence and self-esteem so that they can meet the challenges ahead of them.

Overall, the Logan School attributes its success in environmental problem solving to

(1) the experiential-based component,
(2) the reflection process after an activity, and
(3) the emphasis on creativity and unique ways of approaching problems.

Field experiences give a personal dimension to a student's understanding of a problem that is impossible through a book or lecture. The EE program emphasizes recording and journal writing so that students can synthesize and evaluate something they have just performed. It is essential for them to extract what they have learned as they go, instead of just rushing through and moving on to the next thing. The Logan School believes that problem solving is not reduced to a formula. It is the creativity behind the solutions that make them work. The school provides opportunities for students to develop their creative potential. The EE program supports this philosophy and allows plenty of room for students to explore issues of today and those of tomorrow.

A Cooperative Project to Help Solve Social and Environmental Problems

MARTIN OGLE, POTOMAC OVERLOOK NATURE CENTER, VIRGINIA

For the past three years, Potomac Overlook Nature Center in Arlington, Virginia, has participated in a cooperative project with the Sullivan House (a transitional housing unit) and Mt. Olivet United Methodist Church. These three organizations are attempting to look at environmental and social problems in an integrated way.

The three organizations co-sponsored interns who helped with a variety of activities such as recycling drives; a summer concert series at the park, which serves as a joint social event and fund-raiser; gardening; help with transportation and child care for Sullivan House clients; landscaping projects at each location; and education/life skills programs for people at Sullivan House and the church. In addition to these activities, interns helped with work specific to each organization to gain a deeper understanding of the concerns and problems faced by each. Although the interns were a big part of the project, there were many instances in which people from the three organizations worked together without interns. For instance, a joint Earth Day Event was held in 1990 in which people from all three groups worked at all sites and gathered at the end of the day for a meal and music.

The integrated nature of this project is one way in which it differs from most environmental education programs. The structure and philosophy of the project are such that social, religious, and environmental concerns are addressed together rather than as artificially separate entities. As such, the central questions to this effort have become "What are the real needs of the people and the planet?" and "How do we provide for these needs?" This forces us to confront head-on the root causes of almost all modern problems, namely overconsumption of energy and materials and a mindset that causes us to require this overconsumption for our well-being.

The cooperative project has been valuable in that it has built a stronger sense of community between the organizations and has fostered relationships between the people in them. Since the project is set in the context of a society that is extremely specialized and that measures its success on ever-increasing consumption rates, it sometimes seems like a lonely voice with limited outreach. The activities of the project are sometimes overshadowed by the tumult of the fast-paced world of northern Virginia. However, there are at least three reasons that the project could be considered successful:

1. The activities have helped people. Children from the Sullivan House were delighted by the sight of a live owl up close. People enjoyed each other's company at concerts, picnics, and work projects and learned to get more out of life with less consumption. Interns helped Sullivan House clients find apartments to live in. People learned to garden and compost; the produce was donated to a homeless shelter. People benefitted from the program.

2. The project changed people's outlook on life. Some of the interns have said that working with the three organizations affected the direction of their careers.

3. The project has dealt with difficult problems head-on. An integrated approach to problem solving is often preached but seldom practiced. This project attempted to dive into this process, by tackling the concerns of the organizations and the crucial problem of overconsumption.

The project has been worthwhile because it addresses a strong human need: the need to feel a part of something. The project offered the vision of community in which the human condition could be seen as part of the life processes of Earth.

This feeling of community could be best exemplified by a description of a typical concert sponsored by the three organizations. Concerts were held on a grassy field just outside the nature center at Potomac Overlook. Performers were usually local folks or bluegrass groups known to the staff or friends of the Center. While the band set up, families, couples, and other groups filtered in to the park and began to eat picnic suppers on the lawn. Many people, especially children, interacted with each other, and some toured the nature center. Friends set up a donation box and sold lemonade and home-baked goods to help support the musicians and the Sullivan House. When the band was introduced, a staff person described the cooperative effort and encouraged the audience to return to the center's programs. Most of the bands had an excellent rapport with the crowd, inviting choral participation, stopping to point out a nighthawk, and accommodating dancing children down in front. The music ended just before dark, but seldom did the night's activities end there. Quite a few people walked through the center or stayed to talk to friends.

The concert series has become a very popular event. The number of people attending gets larger every year and most come more than once. Musicians have called requesting to play at the concerts for much less than they would normally charge. People have been generous with donations, and on those few occasions when more funds are needed, the three organizations provide them. Many people comment favorably on the park setting and the opportunity to use the nature center. People find in these concerts a chance to enjoy and fulfill themselves by interrelating with other people and nature; all with a minimum of energy and materials consumed. This is an environmental issue, a social issue, and even a spiritual issue all rolled into one.

Teaching Problem Solving Strategies in a University Environmental Studies Program

Lucie Sauvé, Département des Science de l'éducation and Armel Boutard, Département de Physique, Université du Québec à Montréal

In the frame of a 1-year program in Environmental Studies at University of Québec in Montréal, we designed a course entitled "Strategies for Environmental Problem Solving." This course (45 classroom hours with a total 135 hours workload) is taught based on interdisciplinary projects. After a guided exploration of the urban environment, student teams of 4 or 5 identify a problem and carry out a thorough procedure to solve the problem. Workshops are provided to offer the necessary conceptual, theoretical, and methodological background. Finally, the students present and discuss their work; the use of audiovisual equipment and role play is greatly encouraged.

As the projects progress, the following general objectives are pursued:

- To recognize the characteristics of environmental problems: the complexity and multiplicity of the data, the diversity of actors, the influence of underlying values, the collective character of resources involved, etc.

- To know the characteristics of the process for solving such problems: the different steps (identifying the problem situation; investigating, diagnosing, and defining the problem; analyzing and evaluating solutions; designing and carrying out a plan of action; evaluating the intervention; following through and implementing retroactive changes); the uncertainty and risk factors inherent in decision making; the importance of democratic process; etc.

- To know and experiment with various tools and strategies to investigate, analyze, and evaluate environmental problems: environmental and social impact studies, cost-advantage, risk-advantage and risk efficiency analysis, investigative methods, values analysis, values clarification, structures and mechanisms of public consultation, role playing, etc. The case study is presented as a framing method that can include these different strategies.

- To concretely participate solving environmental problems in, with, and for the environment. Some of the urban environmental problems undertaken in this course were fluoridation of drinking water, remnant forest destruction for urban development, and stream pollution around the airport.

This course calls for a global and interdisciplinary procedure. It tackles concrete problems of the local and regional environment. It implies studying and operating in the field. It allows students to make a synthesis of the knowledge and abilities acquired in other courses of the program, courses which have more specific and disciplinary content. It encourages the development of autonomy in the problem-solving process. It creates favorable attitudes toward cooperative learning and democratic living. It tackles the question of values and offers the opportunity to clarify one's own values. It also allows practicing various communication activities (transmitting and receiving a message, discussing, negotiating, convincing, etc.). This whole set of characteristics is unique to this course in the program. Let us finally mention that it was taught by team teaching involving two professors, one a specialist in biophysical sciences and the other a specialist in the didactics of environmental education.

Evaluation concerns both the problem-solving procedure itself (the project of each team) and the learned content in relation with the general objectives mentioned above. Emphasis is put on a formative evaluation throughout activities. A summative evaluation assesses the final written report and the in-class presentation.

At the time of writing, this course has been taught once. However, the results of this experiment proved satisfactory. There was very high student satisfaction with the course. Through several formal evaluations and our own questionnaires, all the students recognized the importance and significance of such a course; 85% maintained that they learned more than in most other courses of the program. The main criticism was that the workload was too heavy. In addition, there were no failures and a majority of good grades. The few low grades were due, for the most part, to a lack of structuring or completing the final written report, and not to the procedure or the results of the students' research.

Our observations allowed us to notice a great motivation on the part of the students. They took over "their" problem and developed a feeling of responsibility toward its resolution. They felt satisfied by working on a real problem, by becoming specialists of that problem, and by being socially helpful. Most accepted working more hours than the number suggested. An atmosphere of enthusiasm and happiness that prevailed during the final presentation periods equally affirmed the interest of the students.

In conclusion, we consider that the success of the course can be attributed to the following key elements:

- The students' personal involvement in solving a problem of their choice,

- The challenge of contributing to a real problem solving process with the participation of the other actors in the environment, and

- Team work and group support that created an effect of synergy.

Success Stories from Puget Sound:
The Public Involvement and Education (PIE) Fund

ROBERT STEELQUIST, PUGET SOUND WATER QUALITY AUTHORITY, WASHINGTON

In 1985, faced with mounting water quality problems and fragmented jurisdiction and regulatory approaches to managing Puget Sound, the Washington State legislature formed the Puget Sound Water Quality Authority (PSWQA). The authority's task was to create a management plan for Washington's preeminent estuary and its 16,000 square-mile watershed. The plan was to focus public policy and funding resources and to identify roles for local governments, state agencies, Indian tribes, nonprofit organizations, and industry in a way that would recognize the interests of each and coordinate regulatory and nonregulatory efforts to clean up and protect Puget Sound. Because 3.2 million people inhabit the Puget Sound region, it was clear that education would play a key role in affecting needed changes—both for institutions and individuals.

In 1987, the legislature appropriated $1.1 million to create the PIE Fund—one component of the Puget Sound Water Quality Management Plan's education strategy. The PIE Fund is based on several assumptions that are also central to the theory of environmental education problem solving:

- Problems and issues can be identified by the learner;

- Various interests reflect legitimate, unique, and often complementary approaches to problem solving;

- Durable behavior changes result only when individuals or organizations understand their responsibilities and act on them out of their own interest; and

- To be effective, educational programs must lead to tangible results that protect or improve the environment.

Since 1987, $3.3 million have been appropriated to the program, resulting in about 140 PIE Fund projects carried out by a wide range of individuals, organizations, and local and tribal governments. PIE Fund is, by far, the largest single commitment of public funding to environmental education in Washington. With the 1991 adoption of the Puget Sound Water Quality Management Plan as the nation's first adopted Comprehensive Conservation Management Plan under the EPA-administered National Estuary Program, the PIE Fund became a model for other estuary programs. It has subsequently been adopted and modified in at least four other estuary programs as an effective tool for environmental education.

The PIE Fund operates as a contracting program (as opposed to a grants program) in which contractors compete for funding by submitting proposals in response to an agency request for proposals twice each biennium. Proposals must include projects or programs that focus on some issue involving water quality in Puget

Sound (and identified in the Puget Sound Water Quality Management Plan). Each proposal must clearly define a local problem that can be influenced through educational processes. It must identify audiences and expert advisers who reflect the full range of interests and expertise in the problem. The programs must provide information and tools for action—personal or institutional—so that behavior, not just awareness, changes. Finally, projects must establish a concrete link to results measurable in the environment.

An education program is sometimes a microcosm of a larger environmental issue. In many issues, interested and conflicting parties have no opportunities to solve problems together until it is too late: a regulation is being adopted, a project is on the docket for regulatory approval or denial, or it is too late for opposing sides to exercise flexibility, abandon entrenched positions, or effect creative compromise. As a result, opposing "camps" have no shared history of success at compromise and problem solving.

PIE Fund projects all have advisory groups in which traditionally opposing viewpoints must be reconciled so that programs reflect a wide range of interests. PIE Fund operates under the principles that everyone has an interest in clean water and projects must move beyond the "us and them" mentality. In some projects, "odd couples" are forced together to design and carry out the PIE Fund project. These may include industrialists and environmentalists, Indian tribes and sportsmen, and local governments and state agencies. The process of agreeing on what constitutes the problem and formulating an education strategy to solve it is often the first opportunity conflicting groups ever have to collaborate. Many PIE Fund projects leave a legacy of not only the project and its products, but of a fledgling working relationship and experience of trust and effective communication.

For environmental education to be effective, appropriate behaviors must endure beyond the immediate scope of an educational program. Given the principle that everyone has an interest in water quality, durable changes in behavior occur when they also advance the self-interests of the learner. An underlying theme of Puget Sound Water Quality education strategy is that the role of a government agency is to help prioritize issues in terms of benefits and harm to the public interest, mobilize public resources, and provide accountability for achieving desired outcomes—in other words, provide a support structure for citizens themselves to participate actively in solving environmental problems. The PIE Fund assumes that citizens and organizations can solve many of Puget Sound's problems, given assistance and resources. Experience has shown that, in fact, given the resources, as well as encouragement, many PIE Fund projects produce new, unexpected, and often subtle incentives for reinforcing behavior.

For example, one PIE Fund contractor, the National Association of Industrial and Office Parks, was recognized nationally with an environmental excellence award for its publication and video on the use of grass-lined swales for stormwater treatment in developed areas. The effect of the award on the individual developers has been one of reinforcement—they found solutions and were given appropriate credit. The stormwater protection measures that they prescribe for their peers are their own product, not something imposed by government. Most important, these individuals are now viewed as leaders in their industry.

Protecting and enhancing water quality in Puget Sound is the stated aim of the PIE Fund program. For many educators, concrete outcomes represent an insurmountable obstacle, thus we settle for indicators of changes in awareness, knowledge, attitudes, or skills, hoping that such changes will lead further. Information, however, is only an instrument. Informed actions are only means to another set of ends. Defining those ends in clear and measurable terms presents PIE Fund contractors with their greatest challenge. One project focused on nonpoint pollution within a watershed. The test of the effectiveness of their education program was a stream monitoring program that measured nitrogen levels in the water. Indeed, after an extensive program of storm-drain stenciling, the production of a homeowner's guide to the watershed, and extensive classroom programming within schools, measurable levels of nitrogen in the stream declined. In another program, an unexpected outcome of the project was the acquisition and protection of a wetland habitat by the state wildlife agency. The agency purchased the property because of a wetlands education project initiated by a school district and community education center, both of which used their own adjacent wetland properties as part of the PIE Fund wetlands education project.

Not all PIE Fund projects succeed in producing measurable improvements in Puget Sound water quality. However, establishing clear links between desired behaviors and tangible results contributes to clearer objectives and greater overall effectiveness in environmental education programs. Critically, the achievement of real results emboldens program participants—teachers and learners—in tackling new environmental challenges.

For more information about the Puget Sound Water Quality Authority's PIE Fund, contact: Puget Sound Water Quality Authority, PO Box 40900, Olympia, Washington 98504–0900.

A Local Landfill Issue: Strategies for Developing Environmental Problem-Solving Skills

ALICE STEINBACH, BEACH MIDDLE SCHOOL, MICHIGAN

Each year, I seek a local environmental issue to be used as a model for environmental problem solving. Students must become aware of the issue, gain information, and participate in simulations that deal with possible solutions. Before selecting their actions, students become involved as environmental political activists, community educators, or agents for changing behaviors.

In the spring of 1989, we focused on the community landfill. For several months, classes followed media coverage of the Michigan DNR concern that the local sanitary landfill was unsafe and should possibly be shut down. There were many heated meetings between the Chelsea Village Council and DNR officials. We read and posted newspaper articles and letters to the editor in the classroom. An environmental health specialist from the county Department of Health was a guest speaker. He shared the findings of the department regarding leaks of toxic substances reported to have appeared in wells adjacent to the landfill. We arranged field trips to the landfill. Both the local landfill manager and DNR officials were present and helped us understand how landfills operate and what the concerns were at the site. Students also saw how the site related to adjacent private property and state-owned wetlands.

Next, each student, individually or in a group, worked on an independent project. Each project was chosen with consideration for interests, talents, and abilities of the individuals. They included letters to government officials and editors of local newspapers; posters urging the community to recycle and eliminate unnecessary solid and toxic wastes; children's stories about toxic and solid waste concerns; political cartoons; involvement in recycling and using alternative, nontoxic substances in school and at home.

We used aerial photographs of the landfill site and surrounding area for an in-class simulation. Groups of students developed a land use plan for the sanitary landfill site if and when it closed. The plans chosen as "best" by student "village council" members were presented at a Village Council meeting. Members of the Village Council listened to the proposals with interest and asked the students to leave their plans for consideration. The community has since implemented recycling programs for solid and toxic waste.

Thirty years of living and teaching in this community has given me opportunity to interact with and observe students. Today, many former students are employed in environmentally related jobs and professions. Community involvement in recycling, and providing environmental experiences for children, is high. Voting patterns related to environmental issues are positive. Former students contact me for environmental information or to discuss what has happened to "their" issue. Many of my current students are their offspring. They refer to environmental activities in which their parents participated as students. These parents have been supportive of environmental problem solving activities in classes and frequently become involved themselves.

About the Authors

Janet Carrier Ady coordinates environmental education and training programs for the U.S. Fish and Wildlife Service from the Washington, D.C., office. She worked in the Alaska Regional Office from 1983 to 1990.

Janis Albright-Burton has developed and implemented educational programs at the Manomet Bird Observatory in Manomet, Massachusetts, for 11 years.

Lisa V. Bardwell teaches in the Environmental Studies Program at the University of Michigan and works with the National Consortium for Environmental Education and Training in Ann Arbor, Michigan.

Ivan Baugh is a technology teacher in the Louisville, Kentucky, schools.

Armel Boutard teaches in the Département de Physique at the Université du Québec Montréal in Montréal, Québec, Canada.

Anne Camozzi runs EcoLogic, an environmental education consulting firm in Antigonish, Nova Scotia, Canada.

Michael J. Cohen has directed Project NatureConnect for 4 years in Friday Harbor, Washington. Before that he directed the National Audubon Society's Expedition Institute Program for 26 years.

Peter Blaze Corcoran has taught environmental education at College of the Atlantic, Swarthmore College, and is currently chair of the Education Department at Bates College in Lewiston, Maine.

Carol Fialkowski directs the educational programs at the Chicago Academy of Sciences in Chicago, Illinois.

William F. Hammond recently retired as Director of Environmental Education for the Lee County School District in Fort Myers, Florida, is President of Natural Context conducting international Environmental Education consulting work and is a Doctoral Candidate at the Simon Frazier University in Burnaby, British Columbia.

Harold R. Hungerford is semi-retired as the Coordinator and Professor of the Science Education Faculty at Southern Illinois University in Carbondale, Illinois.

Ruth Jacquot directs the Environmental Education Center at Murray State University in Murray, Kentucky.

Dan Kowal is the Environmental Education Specialist at the Logan School in Denver, Colorado.

Martha C. Monroe is on the staff of the National Consortium for Environmental Education and Training in Washington, D.C.

Martin Ogle directs the educational programs at the Potomac Overlook Nature Center in Arlington, Virginia.

Ian Robottom is Associate Professor and Director of Center for Studies in Environmental Education, Faculty of Education at the Deakin University, Victoria, Australia.

Lucie Sauvé teaches in the Département des Science de l'éducation at the Université du Québec à Montréal in Montréal, Québec, Canada.

Eric Sievers attended Swarthmore from 1988 to 1992. He is currently in Kazahustan as a consultant for ISAR, a clearinghouse on grassroots cooperation in Eurasia.

William B. Stapp recently retired from the School of Natural Resources and Environment at the University of Michigan in Ann Arbor, Michigan.

Robert Steelquist is an environmental planner for the Puget Sound Water Quality Authority in Olympia, Washington, and administers the Education and Public Involvement Program, which includes the PIE Fund.

Alice Steinbach taught middle school students in Chelsea, Michigan, for 28 years.

Margaret T. Tudor directs the Education Program at the Washington State Department of Wildlife in Olympia, Washington.

Trudi L. Volk is an Assistant Professor teaching in the Science Education Department at Southern Illinois University in Carbondale, Illinois.

Arjen E. J. Wals teaches in the Department of Agriculture Education at Wageningen Agricultural University in The Netherlands.

Austin Winther is a doctoral candidate at the Southern Illinois University.